Birds of Prey and Owls in Europe

HENK VAN DEN BRINK

REBO
PRODUCTIONS

© 1997 Rebo Productions, Lisse, The Netherlands
© 1997 Published by Rebo Productions Ltd.
Text: Henk van den Brink
Translation co-ordination: Euro Business Translations, Bilthoven, The Netherlands
Cover design: Ton Wienbelt, The Hague, The Netherlands
Picture research: Marieke Uiterwijk
Editor: Elke Doelman, TextCase
Layout: Signia, Winschoten, The Netherlands
Typesetting: Hof&Land Typografie, Maarssen, The Netherlands

Editing, production and general co-ordination:
TextCase Boekproducties

ISBN 1901 094 715

Contents

Preface

Bird lovers nearly always have birds of prey at the top of their list of favourite birds. Sightings of birds of prey species are proudly recorded in field trip journals – which would not be complete without them. Places where concentrations of birds of prey can be found during migration act as a magnet for bird watchers, who travel from far and near to visit them. What is it about birds of prey that fires our imagination so strongly? One of the reasons is probably their rarity. It is a fact that people are more fascinated by the unusual than they are by the mundane, and birds of prey – at least most species of them – are not something you see every day. They are at the end of the food chain, so it is not surprising that there are far less of them than the animals which they eat. Another part of their fascination lies in their aerial skills. That's the special thing about birds of course, that they can fly, and which birds are more skilled at this than the birds of prey? From the vultures that glide on the wind for hours at a time, effortless to all intents and purposes and without a single wingbeat, to the Peregrine Falcon and the hobby, which can achieve speeds in excess of 95 mph (150 kph) or more when swooping on their prey.

There's no denying the sensational quality of the hunt itself, of course, although it must be said that birds of prey when hunting are not always spectacular and can even be a little boring at times. You really do have to spend an awful lot of time in the field before you get to see any decent amount of action, and you can consider yourself very lucky indeed if you see a hunt that is actually successful. But apart from the dramatic aspects, the lives of birds of prey are interesting enough in themselves, as this book may possibly help to make clear. Birds of prey and their nocturnal counterparts, the owls, are portrayed here in their natural environments and in their role as predators and carrion eaters. This is a role which has often been misunderstood, and that still is. This book is not about identifying birds of prey in the field – there is a wide range of guides available for this purpose, both general birdwatchers' guides and books devoted specifically to birds of prey.

Henk van den Brink

CHAPTER I

Introduction

Today, birds of prey incite admiration in many people, but it is not so long ago that the situation was very different indeed. The mutual history of humanity and birds of prey is marred by hate, prejudice and attempts on the part of human communities to wipe these birds out. People took exception to birds of prey catching living animals – not flies or worms, because nobody minds about them, but doves, chickens and rabbits. Until well into the twentieth century, birds of prey were inevitably portrayed as evil beings and exterminated in the same manner as vermin. They have paid a high price for this ruthless persecution over the course of the centuries: most species used to have a much wider range than they do at present, and some of them have been brought to the brink of extinction.

Female Montagu's Harrier.

Right: the buzzard is the most widespread and numerous bird in Europe.

Owls, on the other hand, have not suffered as much, although they have not entirely escaped persecution by the human race. People's attitudes towards owls are not so much characterised by hate as by fear and superstition. Owls are mysterious, shadowy beings. Their nocturnal lifestyle, their silent flight and the strange noises they make lead them to be associated with the powers of darkness, witches, ghosts and enchanters. The quavering cry of the Tawny Owl, for example, is a well-known component of horror films. On the other hand, however, owls frequently inspire feelings of affection, which are equally irrational in their origins. They don't look like bloodthirsty pirates and their somewhat rounded shape even makes them appear "strokeable". Their upright posture and broad

Right: like most owls, this Long-eared Owl mainly hunts at night.

Below: the Barn Owl: shadowy being, subject of fear and superstition, but also bearer of wisdom.

head with the eyes directed towards the front, making it look like a face, imbue them with human qualities, an impression which is intensified by the fact that they have been associated with wisdom since ancient times.

Owls are generally considered to be 'the birds of

prey of the night', and the other birds of prey are sometimes termed 'diurnal birds of prey'.

It is true that their habits exhibit many parallels and owls really are in many respects the nocturnal counterparts of birds of prey. All owls and most birds of prey are predators, which is to say that they are specialised in the capture and killing of living animals. They sometimes hunt the same prey, such as small rodents and songbirds, often in the same territory. They have neatly arranged matters between themselves: birds of prey hunt during the day and owls during the night, though the division is not a razor sharp one. Some birds of prey continue to hunt during twilight, which is when many owls have also started to scout for their dinner. And some owls look for food during the day as a matter of course, such as the Short-eared Owl and the Little Owl.

There are also similarities in their appearance which are connected to their lifestyle. Both birds of prey and owls have a curved beak and powerful toes with fiercely curved nails. But apart from these and a few other superficial similarities, ther are a greater number of differences. The beaks of owls, for example, when examined more closely, turn out to be constructed in quite a different manner from those of birds of prey, exhibiting a greater downward curvature. And birds of prey lack the membrane that owls can slide over the eye like a sort of extra eyelid (the nictitating membrane or membrana nictitans). There is a difference in the number of primaries and in the digestive system. Birds of prey, for example, have a crop to store reserves of food; owls do not have one, but compensate for this lack by means of a more elastic gullet which enables them to proc-

Below: birds of prey have a crop in which to store food reserves, as this buzzard demonstrates. Owls don't have a crop, but can digest more food at one time.

Following pages: the 'regal' head of the Golden Eagle: admired, feared and hated.

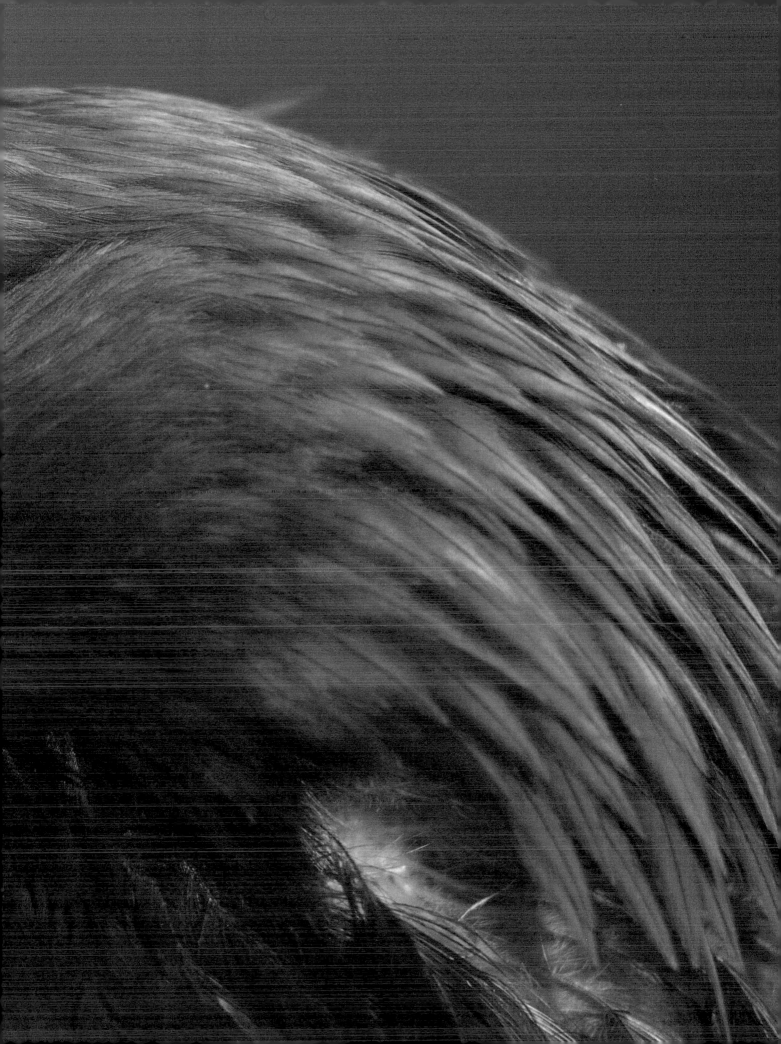

ess more food in one go. These and other internal and external differences have led specialists to conclude that birds of prey and owls are not related at all and that they have no common ancestor.

Owls are related to cuckoos and nightjars, while birds of prey are situated in the classification system of birds between ducks and poultry. Some experts hold the opinion that birds of prey are most closely related to storks. The similarities between birds of prey and owls are a result of parallel evolution, whereby two unrelated groups have developed along the same lines and similar functions have led to similar features.

The same applies, actually, to the group of birds of prey as a whole. While owls form a clearly defined group (order), birds of prey are generally considered to be a collection of three different

With a wingspan of 2.5 to 3m and sometimes a weight of more than 10 kg the Monk Vulture is the largest European bird of prey.

The Sparrow Hawk male is the smallest bird of prey in Europe; he weighs about 150g.

The osprey is a real food specialist.

orders. By far the largest is the Accipitriformes, to which more than three-quarters of the birds of prey belong, including all eagles, vultures, buzzards and Sparrow Hawks. The other two are the Falconiformes, to which the European falcons belong, and the Cathartiformes, the New World vultures or condors. The relationships between the three groups and their evolutionary origins are a little obscure. In formal scientific terms, therefore, a single group called 'birds of prey' does not exist.

In real terms, however, everyone knows what is meant by this. In any case, regardless of how they are classified, birds of prey and owls are extremely successful bird groups.

Right: the Eagle Owl is Europe's largest owl: from 2 to a good 3kg in weight and 160-190cm from one wing-tip to the other.

Both of them display an enormous variety of shapes, sizes and hunting methods – birds of prey more so than owls. The smallest birds of prey and owls are no larger than a sparrow; the largest vultures and condors weigh more than 10kg and measure more than 3m from wingtip to wingtip during flight. Birds of prey especially differ greatly from one another in the shape of the wings and thereby the type of flight they exhibit:

A young Little Owl. The Little Owl is the Owl of Athens, the source of the association of owls with wisdom. It is only a small bird, but not the smallest European owl: that is the Pygmy Owl (55-85g, 35cm wingspan).

An unusual bird with an unusual speciality: the Honey Buzzard.

from the pointed wings of fast-flying falcons to the rounded wings of the manoeuvrable goshawk, and the broad wings of eagles and vultures that enable them to soar so effortlessly. It is this diversity that enables them to feed on a wide range of prey, from insects to deer and antelope, and, as a result, both birds of prey and owls are to be found in all corners of the world, with the exception of the Antarctic and the oceans. They inhabit all types of landscape and biotopes, from the northern tundra to the tropical rain forest. In comparison with the rest of the world, Europe can boast but few species. Of the world's approximately 290 species birds of prey, only 38 (approx. 13%) occur in Europe, and of the world's 130 or so species of owls, 13 (10%) are to be found in Europe. The smallest European bird of prey is the male Sparrow Hawk, that weighs around 150g and has a wingspan of 55cm. The largest is the Monk Vulture, weighing between 7 and 12.5kg and with a wingspan of 2.5 to 3m. The smallest owl is the Pygmy Owl, weighing between 55 and 85g and with a wingspan of 35cm, and the largest is the Eagle Owl, weighing between 2 and 3 kg, with a wingspan of 160 to 190cm.

A young Imperial Eagle. The numbers of this rare eastern-European bird – a different species from the Spanish Imperial Eagle – are declining rapidly. It is on the world list of threatened species.

A male Montagu's Harrier.

Thanks to the greater number of species and variety of shapes, birds of prey draw from a wider range of food sources than do owls. Real gourmets are to be found among the birds of prey, for example, the osprey (a fish-eating hawk), the Honey Buzzard and the Snake Eagle. The names of the latter two indicate their specialisation. Similar types of specialisation are not found in European owls (although in other parts of the world there are fish-eating owls). If owls can be said to specialise in anything at all then it is mice, which constitute a large part of the diet of various species. There are no owls that eat carrion, as do some birds of prey, including the buzzard and the kite. Vultures, on the other hand, are completely dependent on carrion. This difference is not difficult to explain: animal corpses can only be tracked down during the day via the sense of sight (or by the smell, but this is underdeveloped in both birds of prey and owls). This is not possible during the night, when hunting must be by ear, as in the case of owls. Some birds of prey and owls are distributed across almost the whole of Europe (Sparrow Hawk, buzzard, Tawny Owl), others are to be found only in the far north (Gyr Falcon, Snowy Owl), only in the south (Egyptian Vulture) or in the extreme east (Pallid Harrier). Their numbers vary from hundreds of thousands of a very common species such as the buzzard, to less than 200 breeding pairs of a rare, endangered species such as the Imperial Eagle.

In the chapters to follow, I will try to give a systematic description of how the birds of prey and owls that are to be found in Europe live, beginning with the aspect that captures people's imagination the most, whether one approves of this personally or not: the hunt for prey. In the final chapter, I will examine the problematic relationship between the human race and birds of prey and owls.

CHAPTER 2

Built to hunt

The physical characteristics of birds of prey and owls are adjusted to suit their predator lifestyle, to the hunt for living prey. The most important modifications are to be found in the flight apparatus, the sense of sight, the sense of hearing, the feet and the beak. Flying ability plays an important role in the hunt – some form of aerial stunt nearly always precedes the catching of the prey, varying from a brief swoop to a long pursuit. Most species also detect their prey while in the air. Keen perception is therefore indispensable for tracking down prey animals, vision and hearing being the most important senses. The prey is grabbed with the talons, and the majority of species also use the talons to kill it, subsequently tearing it to pieces with the beak.

After the characteristics and features that display adaptation to the hunting method have been discussed, the characteristics of the plumage that constitute an adjustment to other aspects of the birds' lives will be examined: conspicuous versus inconspicuous colouring and patterning; differences in colour between males and females, or a salient absence of these differences; and the moulting of the plumage.

Owls have rather broad, rounded wings. For owls which hunt in open country, like this Short-eared Owl, they are relatively long.

Wings

Birds of prey and owls are masters of the art of flight. This does not, however, mean that they are faster or can outmanoeuvre other birds. Even a peregrine, one of the fastest birds of prey, cannot beat its wings fast enough to keep up with a dove, duck or stilt-bird over any reasonable distance, and no bird of prey can match the acrobatics of the swallow. Birds of prey and owls mainly stand out through their ability to stay in the air for long periods frequently, with relatively little energy consumption. This is due largely to the great amount of lift which they have: the surface of their wings is large in relation to their

Left: the Sparrow Hawk hunts in areas rich in trees and therefore needs to manoeuvre and accelerate. The short and rounded wings take care of this.

Below: his long wings give the Montagu's Harrier a great lift, so that this bird, which hunts in open country, can fly for a long time slowly 'searching'.

body weight. This is immediately evident when you see a bird of prey or owl in the air. Most species are much more impressive when they are flying than when they are sitting in a tree or on the ground.

The amount of lift a bird of prey has varies a great deal from one species to the next and influences the method of hunting. The greater the lift, the slower the bird can fly and the less effort it takes to stay in the air for long periods. It is

Through its enormously long and wide wings the Griffon Vulture can glide through the air, while he scans the ground under him for carrion.

therefore no coincidence that harriers, which track down their prey by criss-crossing areas at a low altitude, have very considerable lift. If a bird has less lift, i.e. is relatively heavier, it can develop more force and speed. This is characteristic of species whose success relies on a lightning-fast attack, such as the goshawk and the Sparrow Hawk.

Apart from the differences in lift, there is a great deal of variation in the wing shape, which is also related to the method of hunting. The goshawk and the Sparrow Hawk have relatively short, rounded wings, which makes them very manoeuvrable. They hunt smaller birds in wooded areas, catching them mainly by means of a brief, rapid attack. Falcons, on the other hand, have narrow, pointed wings that enable them to develop a high speed during normal flight. They hunt in open terrain and do not rely on surprise but simply on pure speed. Birds of prey which are in the air for long periods on the lookout for something edible, such as vultures and large eagles, have long, broad wings and therefore a large amount of lift. Their primary feathers taper towards the tip, giving the wings a 'fingered' look. This reduces air turbulence at

His narrow, pointed wings enable the hobby to reach high speeds.

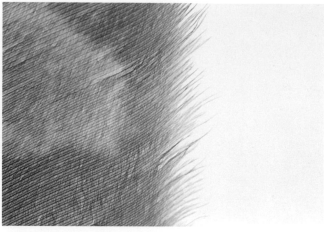

Detail of the flight feather of a Barn Owl.

Left: a flight feather of a buzzard, right: one of a Barn Owl. The hairy extensions which form a soft cover and the downy coverts, enable the owl to fly silently.

A flight feather from a Long-eared Owl. Some owls have 'teeth' on the edges of the feathers, which probably contribute to the silent flight.

the wing tips, thus increasing the upward pressure.

The wing shapes of owls display less variation – all species have relatively broad, rounded wings. Owls which hunt in restricted areas generally have quite short wings (thus increasing manoeuvrability) and those which hunt in open terrain have longer wings (so that they can search for prey slowly).

Owls have a unique characteristic: they can fly without making a sound, something of vital importance for these nocturnal hunters.

This facility not only ensures that prey animals cannot hear an owl coming, but also that the owl itself can pick up the slightest noise.

There would be no point in hunting by ear, paying attention to the slightest rustle, if the noise created by their own wings drowned it out. Soundless flight is made possible by special adaptations of the plumage: the feathers are more supple than those of other birds, and the flight feathers and coverts have a downy edge. These features muffle the sound of the air-stream along and through the feathers.

Vision

Birds of prey hunt primarily or exclusively by sight, and the sense of sight also plays an important role in the case of owls, alongside that of hearing. Both groups therefore have exceptional powers of vision.

Birds of prey and owls see in the same way as do people, i.e. with both eyes straight ahead. This is called binocular vision and it is necessary in order to be able to calculate distances, something a bird of prey on the hunt can't do without. That you need both eyes for this can be tested easily by closing one eye and then trying to estimate the distance to any random point. Other birds see with both eyes to the side, which has the advantage of providing them with a wide field of vision, as much as almost 360° for some species. This is useful for birds, whose main concern is to avoid being caught themselves. Birds of prey actually combine the best of both worlds:

they have two foveas in each eye (humans and other birds have one), which enable them to see both straight ahead and to the side with each eye. Owls have specialised particularly in binocular vision (more than 70°, as opposed to 40° in the case of birds of prey), compensating for the small field of vision which is a result of this with their supple neck. While sitting with their back to you, owls can swivel their heads to look you in the eye.

That owls have very large eyes is something which everybody notices immediately. But birds of prey also have large eyes. The eye of a buzzard, for example, is hardly smaller than that of

Pages 20, 21 and below: owls (Short-eared Owl, pages 20 and 21) as well as birds of prey (Snake Eagle, below) have big eyes, with which they can see excellently. Like humans they have binocular vision: looking straight ahead with both eyes, by which their field of vision overlaps so that they can estimate distances.

This Eagle Owl demonstrates a typical owl trick: looking the viewer straight in the face while having his back to him. The swivelling neck compensates the restricted field of vision.

Birds of prey can also turn their heads far round in order to look around them, as this male Hen Harrier is demonstrating.

a person, and in that same eye are enormous numbers of visual cells, many more than are to be found in the human eye. Visual cells are of two types – rods and cones. Birds of prey have especially many cones, giving them a resolution four to five times greater than that of humans. In the retina of owls it is the rods which predominate.

These are more light-sensitive, and it is thanks to them that owls can 'see in the dark'. If it is absolutely pitch black, owls cannot see anything either, but under natural conditions some light is nearly always present. They have paid the price for this adaptation to their nocturnal way of life by a reduction in resolution, but they compensate for this by means of the large pupil and the greater depth of the eye. The eyes of owls occupy a large portion of the head, enabling them to see very acutely during the day too, just like birds of prey.

Hearing

The extent to which birds of prey use their sense of hearing differs from species to species. Falcons hunt exclusively by sight so their sense of hearing is not particularly well-developed. Harriers, on the other hand, have a very acute sense of hearing, which they use when hunting. This ability to hear the slightest noise comes in very handy since they usually have to search for their prey in long grass, bushes, or other dense vegetation. Birds of prey that hunt in woods and wooded areas, such as the goshawk and the Sparrow Hawk, also use their sense of hearing to track down prey.

But the hearing of these birds of prey is nothing compared to that of owls, which can pick up the slightest rustle. Owls can tell not only from which direction a sound is coming but also how far away it is and at what height. They have very large ears – the head of an owl is all eyes and ears, in fact. The 'ear tufts' of some owls, though, have nothing to do with their real ears, which are hidden behind the facial disk, the ring of stiff little feathers surrounding the owl's eyes. The aperture of the ear is surrounded by movable pleats of skin that can be directed towards the sound, and because of the effect this has on the shape of the facial disk, owls can assume many different expressions. An owl on the alert listening to something looks a lot different from when it is at rest.

Through the mobility of the facial disc, an owl's head (here a Long-eared Owl) can take on various expressions. This is because of the skin pleats behind the ears. The 'ear tufts' have nothing to do with the actual ears. Their real function is not clear.

Claws

Birds of prey and owls grip their prey with their claws, and nearly all species kill the prey with them, not with their beak. Falcons, however, are an exception to this: they can kill with their beak. Birds of prey and owls have strong claws with powerful toes and long, curved nails. The three toes pointing to the front are far apart from each other, ensuring a good grip. Many birds of prey have a long middle toe and a long hind toe, which together act like a pair of pliers. Owls have a rotatable outer toe which can point both forwards and backwards, the so-called reversible toe. They can therefore choose a particular toe formation: three toes in front, one behind, or two toes in front, two behind. In the case of the latter, they have a better grip.

The osprey's foot also has this structure, which certainly comes in very useful when trying to keep a tight hold on its slippery prey. Additional help is provided by the spiny scales on the osprey's toes. Vultures do not have to kill their prey themselves and therefore do not have powerful claws or sharp nails.

Beak

Birds of prey and owls use their beak, the upper part of which curves downwards and ends in a sharp point, to pluck their prey and tear it to bits. In general, the beak is not suitable for killing, although the beaks of falcons constitute an exception to this rule: they have a kind of tooth on both sides of the upper portion of their beak and a depression in the corresponding position of the lower half. Falcons are therefore able to bite their prey very firmly and to kill it using their beak.

Birds of prey have a cere at the base of the beak, a bald area of skin not covered by feathers, where the nostrils are situated. The Honey Buzzard displays a special adaptation for digging out and breaking open bees' or wasps' nests. It is the only bird of prey having a cere that is covered with small scaly feathers to protect it from stings, since this part of the skin is actually rather sensitive.

Colouring

Birds of prey and owls are literally not the most colourful of birds. Owls especially have a very unobtrusive coloration, mostly shades of brown

Previous pages: the ceres of the Honey Buzzard (the part just above the beak where the nostrils are situated), is covered with scales, of a sort which protect this sensitive spot from stings when digging in wasp's nests.

Below: two pairs of claws from Marsh Harriers: strong toes and long, sharp curved nails. The larger claws are from a female, the smaller from a male. In many birds of prey species the female is larger than the male.

What camouflage can do: the Scops Owl looks just like a piece of bark.

Many birds of prey have conspicuous tail patterns.
Incidentally, the male kestrel is one of the most
colourful birds of prey.

and grey, which is in itself not very surprising. The coloration and patterning of birds are not purely decorative – they also have a communicative function. Birds use them as visual signals, for example, to indicate their presence to members of their own species. The males, which are often more colourful than the females, use their colours to impress females and rivals. This kind of 'colour language' would be absolutely useless in owls, which are primarily active at night. This is the reason why male and female owls have a similar appearance.

The patterning of the plumage of owls does, however, serve a very important purpose, albeit quite a different one: camouflage. Owls do not need this during the night, but they do need it during the day, which is when they rest and sleep, and are therefore at their most vulnerable. They try to make themselves as inconspicuous as possible in dense foliage or in compact evergreen trees, often pressing themselves close to the surface of the trunk. They are almost impossible to find there, even if you know where to look, and it is their camouflage which is largely responsible for this. The colour patterning is such that the silhouette of the owl 'dissolves' into its surroundings. This effect is achieved not only through the inconspicuous brown or grey base colour but also and more especially through the various patterns of stripes or patches that are so typical of owls. The colouring of birds of prey is more varied but is still very modest in comparison with most other birds. They do have 'signals' in the form of light wing patches, white rumps and conspicuous tail patterns, but the dominating colours of birds of prey are invariably brown, beige and grey. If they were too brightly coloured their prey would be able to see them more easily.

In some species of birds of prey the males and females differ in colour pattern. The kestrel is one of the clearest examples. Here a pair in a (special kestrel-)nesting-box, the male is on the left.

A conspicuous signal in flight: the white rump of the female Hen Harrier. When she is vulnerable, namely when she is sitting on the ground (on the nest, for example), the spot can't be seen and the bird is simply inconspicuously brown.

Previous pages: the male Hen Harrier is largely light blueish grey. Perhaps the prey animals on the ground don't see him because he doesn't stand out against the sky. The difference in colour is linked to the division of tasks: while the female is brooding, the male brings in the food.

Clear differences in colour between males and females can be seen in harriers, the Sparrow Hawk, the kestrel, the Red-footed Falcon and the merlin. The males of the Hen Harrier, Montagu's Harrier and Pallid Harrier have a greyish blue upper body and the underside is almost white; the females are brown and spotted. There is a reason for these differences – harriers nest on the ground, and the brooding female is inconspicuous there thanks to her protective colour-

Differences between juvenile plumage and adult plumage: photo on previous page and above: the adult goshawk has horizontal stripes on a whitish background; photo right and following page: the breast of a young bird is brown with teardrop-shaped, lengthwise spots.

ing. It is the males that are primarily responsible for providing the food during the nesting period. Due to their light colour they can hardly be seen when viewed against the sky from below, which means that prey animals do not notice them so quickly. The merlin, a small falcon that also breeds on the ground, shows a similar disparity: the female is brown and spotted like the harrier females, and the male has a greyish blue upper body and is pale orange underneath.

A striking characteristic of birds of prey is the great variation in the plumage within a species. The plumage of juveniles generally deviates clearly from the plumage of adults. In the case of larger birds of prey that achieve adult plumage only after a number of years, the juvenile plumage also

Buzzards are very variably coloured. Here a light-coloured specimen.

Here a dark-coloured buzzard.

differs from one year to the next. In addition to these differences determined by age, there are also differences in colour and patterning between adult birds. An extreme example of this is the buzzard, of which both pale and very dark brown specimens are to be found. The Booted Eagle and Eleonora's Falcon have two colour varieties or 'colour phases' – a pale and a dark variety. There are also brown and grey varieties of the tawny owl, both of which are randomly distributed.

Moulting

Bird feathers are subject to wear and tear and must therefore be renewed periodically, in a process called moulting. Many birds moult a large of portion of their plumage all at once. This process, which lasts for several weeks, takes a lot of

energy and is detrimental to the bird's flight capability. For this reason, they hide in dense vegetation during this period, which mostly occurs after the nesting season in summer, when food is plentiful. Birds of prey cannot permit themselves this luxury. They must be able to fly well at all times in order to obtain food and they therefore spread the moulting of the wing feathers (especially the flight feathers) over a long period. Many species moult the whole year round; only during migration does the process come to a halt and, in the case of some species, also during the nesting period. Large species require as much as several years before all the flight feathers have been replaced, and because some of the primaries or secondaries are nearly always in the moulting phase, the wings of large birds of prey often have an irregular, tattered appearance.

Above left and below: the Booted Eagle has two completely different 'colour phases': the light phase (black and white patterned, below) and the darker phase (largely brown, above).

A Red Kite with moulting wing feathers.

CHAPTER 3

Prey and hunting techniques

Birds of prey come in all shapes and sizes, and the spectrum of animals that they eat, together with the hunting methods they have at their disposal to overpower their prey, is equally varied. In the case of owls there is somewhat less variation in all aspects.

A Golden Eagle that whisks a young chamois from a rock face, a goshawk which swoops upon a wood pigeon in full flight, this is the popular image of the way in which birds of prey obtain their food. Many a tall tale tells of birds of prey able to overcome animals far bigger and heavier than themselves. The one about the osprey pulled down into the depths by the huge fish it tried to catch belongs, in my opinion, to the realm of myth, but that birds of prey are sometimes capable of incredible feats is something I would not deny. But not all prey are large, far from it, and not all hunting techniques are impressive. A sobering, perhaps even degrading image is that of the powerful Tawny Eagle sitting on the ground in its winter residence in Africa, enjoying a meal of termites. The same rule applies to birds of prey as to anyone or anything else: why make life more difficult than it has to be?

This chapter takes a look at the different types of prey, whether small or large, and the various hunting techniques of birds of prey and owls.

Hobby

Prey

The following overview will make clear that not only do birds of prey and owls as a group hunt a wide range of prey animals but also that individual species often have a very varied menu. Some of them, such as the osprey and the Snake Eagle, are real gourmets, dependent on a single type of prey animal. The Honey Buzzard is also very specialised but still flexible enough to switch to other food sources if really necessary, expanding its diet to include worms and lizards, eggs and young birds. There are birds which feed solely on insects, such as the Red-footed Falcon, those which eat only birds, such as the Sparrow Hawk and the peregrine, and mice-eaters such as the kestrel, the Barn Owl and the Long-eared Owl. Forming a contrast to these are the less fussy feeders, eating every kind of animal food. The bird having

the widest range of prey is possibly the buzzard, but the kite, the Black Kite and the White-tailed Eagle are close on its heels in this respect.

The Levant Sparrow Hawk, a South-east European breeding bird, eats many large insects such as crickets, grasshoppers and beetles, as well as mice, lizards and birds.

The powerful Steppe Eagle can often be seen on the ground, where, hopping rather clumsily, he stuffs himself with termites and other insects.

Insects

Insects form a part of the diet for surprisingly many birds of prey and owls. These are usually larger insects such as dragon-flies, locusts, crickets and beetles. In the case of the Montagu's Harrier, the Levant Sparrow Hawk, the hobby and the Scops Owl, insects form an important part of the diet. The Lesser Kestrel, the Red-footed Falcon and the Scops Owl even live almost exclusively on insects. All three nest in warm dry areas which are rich in large insects during the summer: the Lesser Kestrel and the Scops Owl in the Mediterranean area, the Red-footed Falcon in the steppes of eastern Europe. The Honey Buzzard is in a class of its own, and is not so much interested in adult bees or wasps but digs out their nests in order to eat the larvae.

Left: The Red-footed Falcon (here a first-summer male) breeds in steppe areas in eastern Europe. His menu consists almost entirely of large insects, which are freely available here in the warm, dry summers.

Below: The Honey Buzzard is, as far as choice of food is concerned, an odd man out among the birds of prey. He digs wasp nests out and eats the larvae.

A food specialist with a dangerous craft: the Snake Eagle.

Worms

This same Honey Buzzard also sometimes eats worms when the opportunity arises, as do other buzzards. The Little Owl and the Scops Owl are expert earthworm hunters, tracking them down in the grass and pulling them from the soil in the same manner as thrushes. Worms, however, are not a particularly important source of food for any bird of prey or owl species.

Amphibians and reptiles

The same applies for amphibians and reptiles, neither forming an indispensable food source.

Many species of birds of prey and various owls occasionally eat frogs, salamanders and lizards but they do not form a substantial part of the menu for any particular species, with one significant exception, the Snake Eagle. The eating habits of this bird are highly specialised, since it lives almost exclusively on snakes, both in winter and in summer. A dangerous specialisation, one might say, the more so when one considers that Snake Eagles are no more immune to snake bites than are other birds or humans. Even so they do very well, thanks to special adaptations such as a loose plumage with long feathers, making it difficult for a snake to bite very deeply, and short, strong, scaly toes. They take a snake with them up into the air and kill it with a bite to the neck. It must take quite a lot of effort to swallow a snake that's still twisting and turning but one or two of them a day seem to be enough for the Snake Eagle.

Fish

The prize for exclusivity goes to the osprey. Ospreys eat only fish, catching them by plunging with outstretched legs into the water of lakes and rivers, sometimes disappearing completely beneath the surface. Everything about this bird – its build, its plumage, its feet – are adapted to this lifestyle. Other non-specialised fish-eaters,

The osprey only eats fish which he has caught himself (by diving into the water).

A fieldmouse: staple food for many species of birds of prey and owls.

for which fish are only one of their many types of prey, are the White-tailed Eagle and the Black Kite. They can catch only fish that swim slowly, close to the surface, and they also eat dead fish floating on the surface or ones that have been washed up on the shore.

Mice and other small rodents

Small rodents, and mice in particular, have the dubious claim to fame of being top on the hit list of prey animal groups of European birds of prey and owls. They are on the menu of all owls and the majority of birds of prey, some species eating almost nothing else. A high toll is taken of a very abundant group, the voles, including the field voles.

The kestrel and the Black-winged Kite are real mice eaters. The Long-legged Buzzard and the Rough-legged Buzzard also live primarily on small rodents. In its north European nesting areas, the Rough-legged Buzzard eats mainly lemmings when they are available. Small rodents (mice, rats) and rabbits are also often on the menu of the buzzard and the Lesser Spotted Eagle, but as many as eight species of owls live primarily or exclusively on mice and voles, for the most part the latter. These eight species are: the Barn Owl, the Hawk Owl, the Tawny Owl, the Ural Owl, the Great Grey Owl, the Long-eared Owl, the Short-eared Owl, and the Tengmalm's Owl. Of the other five owls only the Scops Owl seldom or never eats mice.

Left: The Ural Owl is one of the owl species in the Northern and Eastern European coniferous forests, which live on mice and voles.

Below: The souslik is a marmot-like rodent that occurs in Eastern Europe. It forms an important source of food for birds of prey such as the Saker Falcon.roofvogels zoals de saker.

Birds

After mice, birds are the most favoured victims, and a number of birds of prey are specialised bird eaters. The Sparrow Hawk, the merlin and Eleonora's Falcon have a taste for small birds, mainly songbirds, and the hobby as well as eating insects also eats many small birds. Eleonora's Falcon nests exclusively in the Mediterranean area, mainly on the rocky coasts of islands. It lays eggs only in the summer and the young hatch when the songbirds are just starting to fly south in the autumn. The falcon then hunts the many migratory birds that are crossing the sea, flying past the island or alighting there.

Medium-sized birds, like doves and jays, constitute the food of the goshawk and the Booted Eagle. The peregrine eats birds of this size category too (which includes not just doves but also many types of wading-bird) but it will also take on larger birds such as ducks, poultry and crows. Due to the speed and force with which it swoops on its prey, the peregrine can catch relatively large and heavy birds. Larger birds, such as those

The Eagle Owl is a formidable hunter who is not choosy and even manages to get hold of birds of prey such as goshawks and Peregrine Falcons.

Following pages: The Peregrine Falcon, here 'covering' his prey, is a fast and powerful bird hunter, who can take on birds of quite a size. He eats a lot of ducks and waders.

Below: Widgeons flying up in panic as a Peregrine Falcon suddenly approaches.

Catching adult hares is reserved for the large, powerful birds of prey such as the Golden Eagle and the Eagle Owl.

Left: a Hen Harrier has captured a young rabbit.

of the poultry family, are also the main source of food of the Bonelli's Eagle, the Lanner Falcon and the Gyr Falcon (which also eats rodents). Among the owls there are none specialised in birds, but the Eagle Owl, the Snowy Owl, the Pygmy Owl, the Tawny Owl, the Little Owl and the Short-eared Owl will regularly eat a bird or two. The Eagle Owl is a formidable predator, for not only does it prey on other owl species, it also counts birds of prey such as the goshawk and peregrine among its victims.

Larger mammals

The buzzard and the goshawk can take on prey the size of rabbits. Larger mammals such as adult hares, martens and foxes are the prerogative of large and powerful eagles (the Golden Eagle, the

Tawny Eagle and the White-tailed Eagle) and the Eagle Owl. The Golden Eagle sometimes even strikes at adult deer and chamois, and can kill lambs. Tales of Golden Eagles that kill sheep, however, are pure fiction, probably the result of hastily drawn conclusions after having seen a Golden Eagle eating a sheep. They do eat sheep, but only ones that are already dead.

Carrion

At times during the winter, Golden Eagles live primarily on carrion – dead animals or parts of them. Carrion is also important for the osprey in winter. The kite eats a lot of carrion throughout the whole year, and neither the Black Kite nor the buzzard turn it down. Vultures, which inhabit only the south of Europe, are completely dependent on carrion, feeding mainly on the corpses of sheep, goats and other domesticated animals. They no longer have the strong talons with their firm grip and sharp nails of other birds of prey. The lack of feathers on the head and neck of the Griffon Vulture and the Monk Vul-

Europe's smallest vulture, the Egyptian Vulture, feeds on the remains of carrion left behind by the Monk Vulture and the Griffon Vulture.

Below: After the Monk Vulture, the biggest and strongest species of vulture, has done the rough work, it's the Griffon Vulture's turn to eat the guts of carrion.ingewanden van het kadaver op te eten.

When there is practically nothing left of the carrion than bones, it is finally the turn of the Bearded Vulture. He can digest bone marrow and breaks bones by dropping them onto the rocks.

ty job of slitting open the corpse, then it's the turn of the Griffon Vulture to eat the guts. The Egyptian Vulture, which is much smaller, cleans up the leftovers. And when practically all that is left are the bones and feet, the Bearded Vulture comes into its own. This strange bird likes bone marrow, and smashes bones by flying into the air with them and dropping them on a rock. If there's no carrion around it uses the same method for (live) tortoises, breaking their shell in the same manner.

Flexible feeders

In general, birds of prey and owls are very flexible in their choice of food. They eat whatever is easiest to get – which will depend on its size and their own particular hunting method – and of which there's a plentiful supply at that particular time and place. The Hen Harrier and the Short-

ture are an adaptation to rooting Varound in corpses. There is a definite division of labour between the two: the Monk Vulture, the larger bird with the more powerful beak, does the heavy du-

Birds of prey are flexible in their choice of food. The kestrel might be known as a mouse specialist, but he is not above taking carrion if it suits him.

The Little Owl is not fussy. His diet includes insects, worms,
snails, mice and songbirds.

eared Owl feed mainly on mice, but can switch
to birds with no trouble, especially during the
winter. The Gyr Falcon and Snowy Owl eat a lot
of lemmings but if there aren't very many of them
they turn their attention to ptarmigan and other
birds. In Finland and Russia goshawks live
mainly on poultry species, which are the most
numerous 'catchable' species there. In the case
of western European goshawks the prey mainly
consists of doves, jays and starlings. The list of
prey for each species varies therefore depending
on the place and the time of year.

How birds of prey attune themselves to the pre-
vailing conditions is beautifully exemplified by
the prey lists of goshawks in the Netherlands.
During the autumn and winter the goshawks live
primarily on pigeons, especially wood pigeons.
At the end of May and beginning of June, young

The goshawk is capable of catching and killing a Grey Heron.

Below: the male (left) and the female (right) of the Sparrow Hawk, each covering their own part of the prey spectrum. The small and light male catches mainly small songbirds such as sparrows and finches, the female catches many thrushes and starlings.

starlings leave their nests and promptly appear on the list in large numbers. In June and July, it's the turn of the young jays to try out their wings and the goshawk shifts its attention to this easy target. The effect of bird migration is also immediately visible in the prey list. When the redwings fly in from the north in large numbers you can be guaranteed to find remains of them, plucked by Sparrow Hawks and goshawks. Another good example is the role of crossbills in the menu of Sparrow Hawks in Drente, a province of the Netherlands. Here, the crossbill is an invasory bird – absent one year and present in great numbers the next. A large invasion of crossbills soon led to crossbills appearing in Sparrow Hawk feather remains. At the peak of the invasion crossbills constituted one fifth of all prey.

Birds of prey are therefore very economical in their habits. They go for the most profitable prey

Below and right: Sparrow Hawks eat many sparrows; they often hunt in and around villages. The hobby primarily hunts above the open fields and thus more often catches songbirds which occur there, such as skylarks and wagtails.

species, the ones that are the most numerous and relatively easy to catch. Prey which is too small is avoided because it is not worth the effort of the hunt, and animals which are too quick and agile are left in peace because it would require too much energy to catch them. Prey which is too large also requires too much effort to catch and kill it. In general, birds of prey eat (much) smaller animals than they could theoretically take on. It is true that species such as the Grey Heron, Short-eared Owl and even peregrines occur on the list of birds caught by goshawks but these are the extremely rare exceptions to the rule. Ospreys have occasionally been recorded catching fish weighing as much as 2-3 kg – more than their own body weight – but usually they catch fish between 300g and 500g. Birds of prey avoid competing for food among

The hobby chooses a high point to be on the lookout for prey.

Next pages: the large Saker Falcon makes use of a combination of speed and surprise. At full speed, while skimming over the ground, he usually surprises his prey.

themselves, though there is a certain amount of overlap between birds of prey and owls in the choice of food within a particular area. This is, however, somewhat compensated by the fact that the birds of prey hunt during the day and the owls during the night. Usually there is practically no overlap in the choice of food between the different bird of prey species inhabiting a certain area. Although the goshawk and the Sparrow Hawk, both bird hunters, often nest in the same area, the goshawk preys on larger birds than the Sparrow Hawk. Both species have divided up the range of birds available even further due to the considerable differences in size be-

The hobby makes his own 'mobile lookout post' in the air, by hovering in one place with flapping wings. Everything moves, except for the head which stays in the same position.

The Black-winged Kite, like the Kestrel, eats mainly mice and hovers a lot. The attitude, with the head slightly hanging down, is characteristic (see also the photo on the following page).

tween males and females. The Sparrow Hawk male weighs approximately 250g, the female 270g; a male goshawk weighs around 700g and the female 1200g. The females of both species therefore catch larger prey than do the males. The hobby and the Sparrow Hawk catch birds in the same weight category but the hobby hunts in more open terrain and therefore catches differ-

ent species (swallows and skylarks instead of tits and finches). An exception to this rule is that several species of birds of prey hunt voles, especially in autumn. But in a good year these are an inexhaustible source of food from which several species can easily profit simultaneously without there being a danger of the source drying up. In bad vole years the birds of prey turn their attention to other sources, each species going its own way. The same pattern can be seen in the owls which feed on voles. Some researchers have suggested that the Tawny Owl and the Long-eared Owl compete directly for food, but there is evidence and opinions are divided on the matter.

Hunting techniques

The range of hunting techniques employed by birds of prey is as equally varied as their choice of food. In the case of owls, there is again much less variation in this respect. Most of the hunting

The characteristic image of a harrier searching for food, patrolling low above open fields. This immature male Hen Harrier is changing his juvenile plumage for the blueish-grey of an adult male.

The mice eaters are usually slow and rely heavily on the surprise element. The kestrel, the buzzard and the Rough-legged Buzzard choose a lookout post at a strategic point: in a tree, on a pole or on a rock. From here, they survey their surroundings and nothing slips their gaze. They wait patiently until a prospective prey animal comes along and then they plunge to catch it with a brief swoop. Most owls also use this tactic. If no suitable lookout post is available, some birds of prey create a virtual one by hovering in the air in one position. The kestrel uses this technique especially frequently. If you look at a hovering kestrel very closely you will see that it keeps its head motionless in one position while every other part of its body is moving.

techniques are essentially based on two elements, surprise and speed. In the one species the emphasis is on the surprise aspect and in another on speed.

The Short-eared Owl often occurs in the same areas as the Hen Harrier and, just like him, hunts by flying low over terrain and searching.

The merlin, the smallest falcon and a real bird-eater, also surprises his victims by flying low over the ground and grabbing them after a short and fierce pursuit.

Below: The streamlined hobby is a real open air hunter. While diving he manages to reach a speed of 95-125m.p.h. 150-200k.p.h. and falls precisely onto his target (a songbird).

The buzzard, the Rough-legged Buzzard, the osprey and the Snake Eagle also hover regularly as do the Barn Owl and the Hawk Owl. The surprise element is also a main factor for harriers which patrol the field close to the ground. They scour the surroundings, flying slowly so as not to whizz past any prey that they might locate – quite slow, inattentive prey animals that they can catch immediately. This method is typical for species that eat small rodents and birds. The long-winged owls of the open field such as the Snowy Owl and the Short-eared Owl also hunt in this manner.

Falcons such as the Lanner Falcon, the Saker Falcon and the merlin also hunt while flying low over the ground, but it is speed which is of the essence in their method, rather than surprise attack: the victims see the falcons swooping on them only in the very last moment, when it is often too late.

Surprise is also the main weapon of the goshawk and the Sparrow Hawk, which hunt birds in country with plenty of cover.

When they have a prospective victim in their sights, they approach it stealthily, flying low behind a wooded bank or through a ditch. They appear at the very last moment, hurling themselves on their completely surprised victim, and must grasp it before it has got up full speed in its attempt to escape, since most of the birds they prey on can fly faster over longer distances.

The ones most dependent on pure speed are the peregrine and hobby, both of which hunt birds on the wing in open terrain. They search for suitable prey from a lookout post in a treetop or a rocky ledge, or while circling in the air. When they have targeted it they draw in their wings and plunge towards it like a torpedo. If the target is not below the bird of prey but at the same height, it climbs considerably before initiating the swoop. The peregrine can achieve speeds of 200-300k.p.h. during such a swoop

and the much smaller, lightweight hobby can manage 150-200k.p.h. The swoops are executed over large distances, mostly between 500 and 2500 metres (although swoops of 4-5km are not unknown), and are accurate to within ten centimetres.

Above: large and small pray: the nest of a Hen Harrier with a rabbit and a dwarf shrew (plus a pellet, right).

At the approach of a bird of prey, waders form a compact group which carry out fast flying manoeuvres as one.

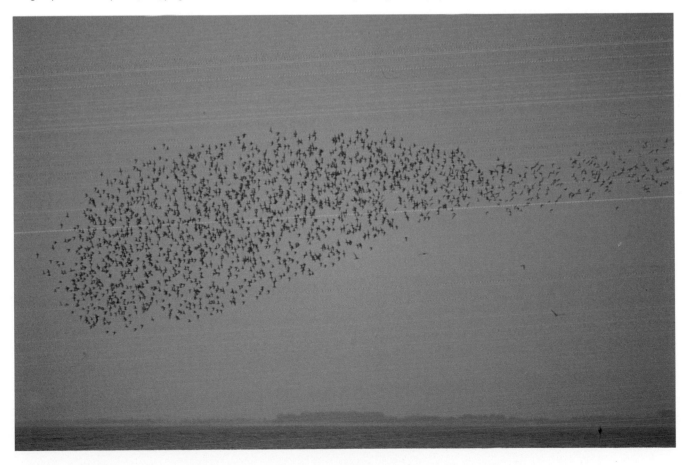

A slight elevation in the terrain is often chosen for plucking prey.

Pellet of a harrier

The hobby often combines this hunting method with the strategy of the goshawk and Sparrow Hawk by executing the last part of the strike almost horizontally under cover. The other way round, goshawks and Sparrow Hawks sometimes hunt in the same way as the peregrine and the hobby by performing strikes from a great height and over great distances.

As you can see, even quite specialised birds of prey are flexible in their hunting methods, and species with a varied menu such as the buzzard, kite, Black Kite and most eagles are even more so. Their hunting strategy is difficult to describe in a few words, though one word does capture it quite succinctly and that is the word 'opportunistic'. These birds avail themselves of different techniques depending on the situation. They search patiently for food and lie in wait, or they fly around, hunting any prey they happen to startle; then follows a brief swoop, a longer swoop, or a surprise attack, with the victim being grabbed on the ground or in the air – every species has several options open to them.

Not all hunting techniques are strenuous and spectacular – birds of prey often use very 'cheap' methods in order to get something to eat. Catching insects is a particularly lazy method and carrion-eating even more so. Some birds steal young birds from nests, as do crows, sometimes even from other bird of prey species and occasionally from their own!

The Egyptian Vulture can break eggs by dropping them on stones or by dropping stones on the eggs, which makes it one of the select group of animals that use tools. Another cheap method is piracy, robbing other birds of prey of their recent catch. Ospreys and kites regularly practise this method with quite a degree of success, but many other species have also been seen to do this sometimes.

Hunting success

Not every attempt of a bird of prey strikes home – on the contrary. The percentage of successful strikes is usually low, often below 25 percent. Higher percentages have been recorded, but they depend on the circumstances and vary according to time and place. That it takes a lot of effort for a bird of prey to book a successful catch is not that unusual because, after all, prey animals don't just sit there waiting to be caught. They have developed all sorts of strategies to make life difficult for their attackers. Some are just too fast, others hide themselves too well. Voles and mice reduce the risk of being caught by their diurnal rhythm. Every two hours all of them at once become active for a while; the rest of the time they sit safely underground. The swarming habits of many birds outside the nesting season also serves to reduce the chance of being caught as much as possible.

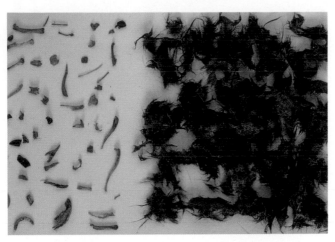

The contents of the pellet: mouse fur, jaw (lower) and other bones of a field mouse, and beetle wing cases.

It's more difficult for a bird of prey to hunt a large group than it is to hunt an individual bird. A group of starlings attacked in flight by a Sparrow Hawk forms a compact 'ball' by flying very close together. The Sparrow Hawk's strategy is aimed at isolating one bird from the group and this can be seen regularly at the roosting sites of starlings.

This may give the impression that birds of prey have to work hard for their meals, but it is really only one side of the coin. The amount of effort they have to expend does not, after all, depend only on the amount of effort required for a single catch but also on the number of catches they need to make in order to fulfil their daily nutritional requirements, i.e. the size of the prey is important also. A buzzard needs 5 or 6 mice or voles a day but if it catches a rabbit that's it for the day. A goshawk that catches a well-fed wood pigeon has more than it can eat in one day. For the rest of the time, therefore, it can rest on its laurels, something which birds of prey will always do, given the chance.

Digestion of the prey

Insects are swallowed whole immediately on being caught. Other prey is first taken to a quiet place, on the ground, or an elevation such as a tree stump, or to a tree. Birds of prey ingest small prey animals whole. Larger prey is first divested of inedible parts by the beak and then torn into smaller pieces. If the prey is a bird, the feathers are systematically plucked, which results in a circle of feathers being left behind that is primarily characteristic of the feather remains of the goshawk and Sparrow Hawk. Stomach and intestines (often including plant material) are removed and some of the bones are also left behind – the larger the prey the more bones are left. The prey is eaten one piece at a time.

Owls do not go to so much trouble. If they can, they swallow the prey skin and all, the selection of what is and is not digestible taking place in the intestines. The non-digestible parts are regurgitated via the beak in the form of a compact ball of fur, feathers, bones and suchlike, called a pellet. Since owls often have fixed feeding places, it is possible to collect the pellets of an individual owl systematically. In this way one can learn a lot about the composition of its food and this is sometimes surprisingly informative with regard to the animals it preys on. Pellet studies have, for instance, indicated the presence of mice species in locations where they were previously thought to be absent.

The Long-eared Owl eats primarily mice, especially field mice.

CHAPTER 4

Birds of prey, owls and their prey animals

The role of birds of prey and owls as predators and their influence on prey animals is persistently misunderstood. Many people still believe that birds of prey form a threat to the levels of the animals they prey on. Some even believe that they could lead to the extinction of their prey or their disappearance from certain areas. This is a distorted view of the situation, one that has led to their persecution by the human race, both in past centuries and even today, making considerable inroads on the bird of prey population. In this chapter I will try to change this image of birds of prey as rapacious thugs.

Poisoning by non-degradable pesticides led in 1970 to a significant drop in the Sparrow Hawk population throughout the whole of Western Europe. When use of pesticides such as DDT was banned the Sparrow Hawk made a tremendous recovery. The population of songbirds such as finches, starlings and sparrows, the prey of the Sparrow Hawk, did not change noticeably throughout all this.

No real threat

In the polders of the IJsselmeer, in the Netherlands, during the first few years after the land had been reclaimed, there were plagues of field mice which attracted large numbers of harriers, Rough-legged Buzzards and Short-eared Owls. In the 70s, the abundance of mice in the recently reclaimed Lauwersmeer was responsible for a large increase in birds of prey in that area. In the early 90s there was an enormous increase in the numbers of mice in fields in East Groningen that had been left fallow, resulting in an influx of many birds of prey. The population of mice eaters such as the kestrel and the Long-eared Owl follows the pattern of mice cycles: good mice years ensure large numbers of kestrels and Long-eared Owls and in bad years their numbers decline. In park-like areas with lots of songbirds, Sparrow Hawks nest in greater densities than in monotonous coniferous woods on poor quality sandy ground. In fertile low-lying country with a

The female Montagu's Harrier with a shrew that she has grabbed from the vegetation with such force that a whole tuft of grass has come along with it.

Female Montagu's Harrier with a shrew in her talons.

large palate of food options, more buzzards nest than in sparsely vegetated mountain areas.

All these examples show that the numbers of birds of prey are determined by the available food. The number of prey animals determines the number of birds of prey, not the other way round! Actually this is quite logical if one applies the same principle to other animals. Blackbirds are to be found in places with lots of earthworms, if the air is thick with insects there also are swallows, and in areas with lots of wild plants there are lots of goldfinches. No-one would seriously postulate that there are hardly any more earthworms because of blackbirds or that no insects are left after the swallows have had their fill or that the goldfinches have led to the disappearance of wild flowers. But when talking about birds of prey this type of non-logic suddenly becomes applicable, although their relationship to their food supply is basically no different.

An unintended experiment with birds of prey in the 60s provided indirect proof for the hypothesis that birds of prey have little influence on the population levels of their prey animals. Through

Mice are not only part of the staple diet of many birds of prey and owls but also of predators such as this weasel. The weasel in its turn also appears on the menu of many birds of prey.

Below: a pair of oyster-catchers attacking a Marsh Harrier. The harrier quite fancies a young bird but the oyster-catchers are not about to give him the pleasure.

poisoning with non-biodegradable pesticides, the populations of Sparrow Hawks, goshawks and peregrines went into serious decline in large parts of Europe within the space of a few years. Although these birds of prey disappeared completely from large areas, there were no reports of large increases in their prey animals (songbirds,

doves). When the situation was reversed, i.e. when the population of birds of prey recovered after the banning of the most destructive pesticides, there was no noticeable decrease in the number of songbirds and doves. Bird counts in Great Britain and the Netherlands showed that the populations of the most important birds preyed upon remained at the same level or even increased.

That the effect of predation is generally limited can be interpreted in various ways. In the first place, the same applies to birds of prey and their food as to blackbirds and earthworms or swallows and insects: the food source is so abundant that that taken by the birds is but a small fraction of the whole. The total effect upon the prey animal population is negligible. Sparrow Hawks and goshawks usually catch no more than a few percent, sometimes much less, of each prey species in their territory. There are exceptions to this rule of course but even then it cannot be

concluded that birds of prey have a negative effect upon their prey animals. Goshawks may well eat half of the young jays in their territory but the jay population remains constant when viewed over a longer period. This is because there are other factors governing the death rate

Above: kestrel

Left: a pair of Hen Harriers with the male in the foreground. The mice plagues in the freshly drained polders of the IJsselmeer attracted great numbers of harriers.

Following pages: a buzzard covered with snow. Getting food is difficult under winter conditions. The main thing then is to use as little energy as possible.

A nest with young kestrels. In years when mice are abundant, kestrels rear many young to adulthood. After bad mice years the kestrel population declines.

Left: young long-eared owls. The mouse population determines the number of Long-eared Owls. After good years there are a lot of them, after bad years only a few.

of young jays that compensate for this. It is possible, for example, that more of the young birds that are left over survive the winter because they are less likely to experience a shortage of food. The life expectancy of the adult birds may also be higher. Another type of compensation is that prey species adjust their rate of reproduction. Songbirds, which are often a target of birds of prey, lay more eggs and produce several broods per year, for example. The same compensating mechanisms ensure that the population of prey animals does not increase if a certain bird of prey disappears. The mechanism can take the form of a high death rate through lack of food, illness or parasites, to name but a few. The prey animals can also react by producing less young, or fewer clutches of eggs per season or by laying fewer eggs. It is extremely improbable that birds of prey (or owls) would cause their prey animals to die out. This is in fact ruled out by the way in which they choose their prey. We saw in the previous chapter that birds of prey always divert their attention to the most profitable prey for them, the prey animals that are the most numerous in their territory at that particular time and that they can catch with relatively little effort. This means that abundant species appear more often on the menu and rare ones less often than their relative numbers would lead one to expect. The fewer there are of a particular prey species, the smaller the chance that it will be caught by a bird of prey.

Supposed usefulness

Some people also do their best to demonstrate how 'useful' birds of prey (and owls) are in order to combat the animosity towards them. By doing so, however, they are showing themselves equally mistaken in their beliefs concerning birds of prey. They proclaim that birds of prey regulate the populations of their prey animals by preventing them from becoming too numerous, but this is overestimating the effect of predation by birds of prey on the numbers of prey animals, which is generally very limited. Apart from this, if predation stops it is compensated by other factors, for example, a higher death rate through lack of food or other causes. This can be seen very clearly in the case of plagues of mice. The numbers of mice are then so great that huge numbers of birds of prey and owls profit from it without thereby reducing the plague to any great extent. The numbers of mice fall later due to other causes.

One also often hears that birds of prey help to keep populations 'healthy'. It is true that weak animals and less fit ones stand more of a chance of being caught, but there is no proof that there are more sick animals walking and flying around in areas with few birds of prey than there are in areas where birds of prey are numerous. Even if that was true, it still does not prove the 'useful-

Jay. Young jays are easy prey for goshawks, which sometimes winnow out half of the nesting period's 'crop'. An exceptionally high percentage, but the jay population does not appear to suffer.

Below: young rabbits are an attractive source of food for many birds of prey. Not without reason is the proverbial reproductive rate of rabbits so great.

ness' of birds of prey. In the case in point, disease takes over the role of predation as the regulating mechanism controlling the numbers of animals – a different mechanism, but not a better or worse one.

Birds of prey are neither 'useful' nor do they constitute a 'threat'. These human concepts are simply not applicable to nature. Birds of prey make up part of a complex of life forms displaying all types of interdependencies, and their feeding behaviour is one of these many interlocking mechanisms. Birds of prey are just playing their part in the whole – neither good nor bad, merely functional.

CHAPTER 5

Birds of prey, owls and their habitats

Birds of prey and owls are to be found everywhere in Europe, in all areas and all types of landscape. But not all species are found everywhere. Each species has its own habitats: different species live in woods than in open countryside and some species favour dry areas, others wetlands. The availability of food, the suitability of the terrain for a particular hunting method, and the presence of nesting and hiding places determine the occurrence of a species. The climate is also an influencing factor, along with the structural features of the landscape. You will find different species in northern Scandinavia than in the Mediterranean area.

A Short-eared Owl's nest

Right: ruins. Suitable nest site for the Little Owl and the kestrel.

In this chapter we will take a look at the most important landscape types and climate zones in Europe together with the birds of prey and owls that live there, looking first at the north and then moving south. Some species are specific to a certain habitat or geographical zone: the osprey is solely to be found in the vicinity of water, and the Gyr Falcon is restricted to the most northern part of Europe. Others are distributed more widely and inhabit an assortment of habitats. The Golden Eagle and the peregrine can be found in all types of open country, from the northernmost point in Europe to the coast of the Mediterranean Sea. The Eagle Owl inhabits both woods and the treeless steppe. Broadly speaking, the number of species increases from north to south, although remarkably enough, this is not true of owls.

This distribution concerns the nesting habitat – in the winter the picture alters somewhat. Some species go to Africa, others move southwards

The Rough-legged Buzzard is a typical inhabitant of the tundra and the Scandinavian mountains (the 'fjell'). It flies more to the south in the winter, keeping to open terrain. There it can easily be photographed, such as here, for instance, on a clod of earth in the middle of a field.

within Europe and some remain in the same area. Species that remain in Europe may inhabit different types of landscape in the winter than they do in the nesting season. Rough-legged Buzzards exchange the Scandinavian tundra for the coast of western Europe; buzzards and goshawks that nest in woods then move out into open country.

Tundra and the Scandinavian mountains

The north of Scandinavia and Siberia is mainly tundra – a vast, treeless landscape with a low cover of grass-like plants, mosses and lichens, and miniature shrubs. In winter the ground is just about completely covered with snow and in summer the subsoil remains frozen (permafrost), leading to the formation of pools and marshes. In the brief summer millions of migrating birds and countless lemmings and other small rodents en-sure a fleeting profusion of food for birds of prey. The rest of the year the supply is rather

A Great Grey Owl is one of a whole range of owl species that nest in the taiga of Scandinavia and Siberia where they live on small rodents, mainly mice.

The Snowy Owl nests in the open tundra of the far north.

thin on the ground. The Scandinavian mountains either side of the Norwegian-Swedish border are a comparable landscape in which the life forms are largely the same, and where therefore the same birds of prey and owls are also to be found.

Birds of prey characteristic of this area are the Gyr Falcon, the Rough-legged Buzzard and above all the Snowy Owl. These three species are restricted almost exclusively to this biotope. In addition to them, the Golden Eagle, the peregrine, the merlin and the Short-eared Owl nest in the tundra but they are not really typical, occurring in greater numbers in other areas and habitats. The Gyr Falcon lives mainly on ptarmigan. These are permanent residents so the Gyr Falcon has nothing to worry about in the winter either and does not need to leave the tundra. The Rough-legged Buzzard is dependent on lemmings and other voles. These are unavailable in the winter, compelling it to migrate to more southern locations. Snowy Owls also live mainly on voles but are flexible enough to switch to other food when necessary, such as birds.

Owls of all shapes and sizes are to be found in the taiga. Even the smallest species, the Pygmy Owl, nests there in holes in tree-trunks.

The goshawk nests in forest throughout most of Europe, from the north to the south, including the taiga. This young specimen was photographed in Finland.

Taiga

At its southern edge, the tundra gradually changes into the taiga – expansive, mainly coniferous forests. The forest is not continuous but is regularly interspersed with peat bogs and marshes, sometimes only tens of square metres in size, sometimes hundreds of hectares. The large open areas are the domain of the merlin, the smallest European falcon that hunts songbirds, and the Short-eared Owl, which lives on both mice and birds. The Golden Eagle, peregrine and Rough-legged Buzzard have also spread to this area and in the southern parts of the taiga, in open areas, the Hen Harrier appears, a bird that nests on the ground like the Short-eared Owl and (usually) the merlin.

As many as five characteristic owl species live in the forests of the taiga zone. The Hawk Owl and the Great Grey Owl are to be found nowhere else; the Pygmy Owl, the Ural Owl and the

Left: another inhabitant of northern forests, especially towards the east: the Ural Owl.

Tengmalm's Owl also nest in mountain forests in central Europe. The Hawk Owl, the Great Grey Owl and the Tengmalm's Owl are dependent on voles for their food supply. These are also on the menu of the Pygmy Owl and the Ural Owl but the Pygmy Owl eats many small songbirds in addition to this and the Ural Owl larger birds and various species of rodents. The Pygmy Owl is the only one to live deep in the forest – the other owls, however, are to be found in the open spaces. That is also true of the birds of prey that live in the taiga. The most widely distributed are the goshawk and the Sparrow Hawk, both bird hunters. The buzzard and Honey Buzzard appear more to the south, the Honey Buzzard preferring dense forest while the buzzard needs open terrain in order to hunt. None of these species is really characteristic for the taiga – all four of them nest throughout Europe, right down to the Mediterranean Sea. In the north they are migratory birds, in contrast to the owls of the taiga, which are permanent residents and only migrate or go wandering in years with very few mice.

Most birds of prey that nest in forests search for food outside of it in open terrain. The choice of hunting territory can be quite varied, as exemplified by this young goshawk.

Forests of the temperate zone

In the mixed forests and deciduous forests of the temperate zone we again meet the Honey Buzzard, buzzard, goshawk and Sparrow Hawk, species with a wide distribution encompassing practically the whole of Europe. Although the other members of their species that nest further north are migratory, here the buzzard, goshawk and Sparrow Hawk are permanent residents. Two species of owl, the Taw-

ny Owl and the Long-eared Owl, are equally widely distributed across all wooded areas. The Lesser Spotted Eagle and the Spotted Eagle are rare summer guests in wooded areas in eastern Europe. None of these species actually lives solely in forests, the Honey Buzzard being their most frequent visitor. The Lesser Spotted Eagle and the Spotted Eagle nest in big forests but often seek their food outside it: the Lesser Spotted Eagle in cultivated landscapes and the Spotted Eagle in marshes and in the vicinity of water. The abundant species (buzzard, goshawk, Sparrow Hawk, Tawny Owl, Long-eared Owl) nest mainly at the edges of forests and are also frequently to be found in semi-open cultivated landscapes where agricultural land alternates with small woods, groups of trees and wooded banks.

Semi-open cultivated landscape of temperate zones

Together with the buzzard, the kestrel is charac-

teristic of this type of landscape, formed by human hands, that has taken the place of the original forest. Kestrels are without a doubt now to be found in more locations and in greater numbers than in prehistorical times. They do not like dense forest, but do occur where the landscape is more open, as long as there are places to nest. This may be a tree, but it could also be a pole, a pylon or a building. The hobby is also characteristic of semi-open cultivated landscapes, being a bird that nests in trees (which may or may not be part of a forest) and hunts other birds in the open field. The hobby also has

The Lesser Spotted Eagle is a rare summer visitor of extensive lowland forests in Poland, the Baltic states and Western Russia.

The Spotted Eagle is even rarer than its little brother, the Lesser Spotted Eagle, and its nesting area lies somewhat more to the east. Like the Lesser Spotted Eagle it also nests in large lowland forests but is more restricted to those with water in the vicinity.

The buzzard nests throughout all wooded areas in the temperate zone. It is not particularly restricted to forest, preferring rather a mixed landscape with forests to nest in and open terrain to hunt in.

a wide distribution but is much less conspicuous and does not occur in large numbers anywhere. A still rarer bird with an more limited distribution is the kite, a bird typical of countryside with rolling hills, fields, and woods here and there. This is where its hunting method, whereby it glides for long periods on its large, long wings, can best be utilised. It is not due to natural causes that the area of distribution of the kite (mainly central Europe) is so small; it is absent from many possible nesting

Right: the kestrel nests in all types of agricultural landscape in large parts of Europe.

Left: a bird that nests in wooded areas in a large part of Europe – the Tawny Owl. It is a hole-nesting bird that prefers mature deciduous forest.

Following pages: nesting biotope of the buzzard and many other birds of prey and owls in the temperate zone: deciduous forest bordering on an open landscape.

areas as a result of persecution. The kite eats carrion and can therefore be poisoned very easily. Together with the Tawny Owl and Long-eared Owl, which prefer wooded areas, the Little Owl and Barn Owl are characteristic owl species of cultivated landscapes. They like more open areas and avoid places where there are too many trees close together, feeling most at home in a small-scale landscape where peaceful meadows, fields and orchards alternate with mice-rich road verges and farms. Barn Owls nest in buildings, especially barns of course; Little Owls nest there too sometimes but they also avail themselves of a whole range of other nesting sites.

Open country of the temperate zone

Harriers are pre-eminently birds of the open country and three species of them are to be found in central and western Europe. The Marsh

Little Owls are present in all types of landscape throughout large parts of Europe. They avoid forests, mountains and open water, preferring small-scale, cultivated landscapes.

The Little Owl selects very varied nesting sites: these may include (open) barns, hollow trees and rocky crevices.

The Hen Harrier breeds in open country, such as the dunes on the Frisian Islands.

The Short-Eared Owl inhabits open country, often in the same sort of terrain as the Hen Harrier.

Mountains

The most characteristic bird of prey of mountainous areas is the powerful Golden Eagle. In Siberia, it also lives in lowland country but it still prefers a biotope consisting of treeless mountains, from Scandinavia to Spain, where it nests on rocky ledges. The other characteristic species of high mountains, the Bearded Vulture has been practically exterminated; the few remaining Bearded Vultures nest mainly in Spain. In the Alps, people have tried to reintroduce the Bearded Vulture by releasing specimens into the wild. Centuries ago, the Griffon Vulture probably also inhabited the mountains of central Europe.

Right: Hen Harriers nest on the ground in thick vegetation, consisting of grass, herbaceous plants or low shrubs. The brown female is inconspicuous in these surroundings.

Harrier is primarily a bird of the wetlands and we will return to it later in this chapter. The Hen Harrier and Montagu's Harrier are at home in drier places. We already came across the Hen Harrier in the peat bogs and marshes of the taiga; the Montagu's Harrier prefers to nest in warm, dry areas and is more numerous in southern and eastern Europe. Both species inhabit mainly non-cultivated areas in temperate zones: peat bogs, moors, the drier parts of marsh areas, and dunes. In these areas we also meet the Short-eared Owl again, in many respects the 'owl version' of the Hen Harrier. Montagu's Harrier also nests in fields but the increasing modernisation of agriculture makes it more and more difficult for it to raise its young.

The Marsh Harrier is a bird of the wetlands. This is a male in a typical breeding habitat.

The osprey lives in a fresh-water habitat the whole year round.

Rocky cliffs are suitable nesting sites for many Southern European birds of prey such as the Griffon Vulture, the Egyptian Vulture, the Bearded Vulture and the Golden Eagle.

Coast

Real sea birds are not to be found among birds of prey and owls, and there are hardly any coastal species. The White-tailed Eagle is often to be found on the coast, but it is also found inland, where it nests in trees and searches for food near lakes. In Europe, the osprey mainly nests inland near freshwater and only the small population of the Mediterranean area is restricted to the coast, as is frequently the case in other parts of the world. In Great Britain, rocky coasts are the preferred biotope of the peregrine; in other countries it inhabits a wide range of biotopes.

The bird of prey most restricted to the sea is the Eleonora's Falcon, which nests on the rocky coasts of islands in the Mediterranean Sea. In spring and autumn it lives on the millions of migratory birds that fly past there. Its nesting season is synchronised to this seasonal fluctuation of its food source: the young grow up in autumn at the high point of the migration of songbirds to Africa.

Water and marshes

One could say that the osprey is the only real water bird among the European birds of prey since it catches its prey in the water, its food consisting exclusively of fish caught alive.

The White-tailed Eagle and the Black Kite catch fish as well, but only slow ones that can be plucked easily from the surface of the water. Neither are they, in contrast to the osprey, averse to the odd dead fish washed up on the beach, and they will also eat other carrion. Although the Black Kite is notable for its lack of specialisation, eating almost all types of animal food, it almost always nests in the vicinity of water.

The Marsh Harrier is a typical wetland inhabitant, preferring to nest in reeds, hidden in vegetation on the ground, just like other harriers. It also finds its food in marshes but occasionally switches to nearby agricultural land.

Mediterranean forests and open country

At one time the Mediterranean area was almost completely covered with forest, of which there are now only a few pitiful remains. This forest looks quite different from northern forests; it is much more open and the trees are lower, displaying more lateral than vertical growth. Human exploitation began early here. Thou-

sands of years of felling, burning off and grazing with sheep and goats led to the creation of open countryside, ranging from the 'maquis' – a thick jungle of low shrubs rich in herbaceous plants – to almost pure desert. Although one could say, in fact, that this was an ecological catastrophe, it probably wasn't such a bad thing for birds of prey and owls, since open or semi-open terrain, which is good for hunting, is actually more attractive than forest for many species.

That having been said, there are more bird of prey species in the Mediterranean area than anywhere else in Europe. Nearly all species that nest in the temperate zone (Honey Buzzard, goshawk, buzzard, etc.) are also to be found here, accompanied by quite a number of other species. This is not only due to the varied landscape – the favourable climate ensures a large and varied range of food and favourable hunting conditions throughout the whole year. Only one species can be added to the collection of owls in the subtropical zone – the Scops Owl.

The bird of prey that feels most at home here in the forest is the Booted Eagle, which looks roughly like a well-built buzzard but is faster and

The Scops Owl is widely distributed in all types of park-like landscapes in the south of Europe. Its penetrating, continuous call can also be heard from twilight onwards in the vicinity of human residential areas.

The Bonelli's Eagle nests in hill and mountain areas in Southern Europe. It builds its nest on rocky ledges.

The East European Imperial Eagle builds its nest in trees but avoids dense forest just as much as bare, open country. Anything in between is suitable, in principle.

The Snake Eagle is mainly to be found in dry, more or less open areas in Southern and Eastern Europe.

more powerful, hunting both birds and rodents. It's big cousin, the Bonelli's Eagle also sometimes frequents the forest but is generally to be found in more open terrain, nesting both in trees and on rocky ledges. The Monk Vulture and the Imperial Eagle nest in trees, often in a forest, but search for their food in open terrain. Monk

Vultures are almost solely to be found in Spain – they have been wiped out just about everywhere else. Griffon Vultures and Egyptian Vultures nest on cliff faces and can inhabit completely treeless areas if necessary. The Snake Eagle and the Lesser Kestrel also prefer open areas. The Snake Eagle nests in trees, the Lesser Kestrel on buildings in villages and towns.

Steppe

Steppe is open, flat or rolling terrain and the vegetation consists primarily of grass. The climate is tough: summers are hot, winters cold, and it is above all extremely dry. Even so, it is the preferred biotope of quite a number of birds of prey. Their food consists mainly of the rodents that are here in abundance, such as souslik, and insects such as locusts and crickets. In Europe, steppe areas used to be confined to the southeast but because of over-exploitation and erosion, savannah, steppe and even desert-like areas have been created in the Mediterranean countries.

Some birds of the steppe have a predominantly eastern distribution. In the extreme east of Europe the Pallid Harrier joins the Montagu's Harrier that we came across earlier but is here more in its element. The Long-legged Buzzard, the Saker Falcon (a large falcon) and the Red-footed Falcon are also typical eastern birds nesting in the steppe; they are mainly to be found in Asia, and in Europe are present only in

The long-legged Buzzard breeds in dry open steppes and savannah like areas of South-eastern Europe.

The Montagu's Harrier nests on the ground in steppe but also frequently in fields.

the extreme east. Another large falcon related to the Saker Falcon, the Lanner Falcon, is more a bird of the desert and is primarily an African species. Within Europe it is to be found mainly in Italy and the Balkans. Strangely enough it does not occur in Spain, although the Iberian peninsula is the only place in Europe where the other African inhabitant of the steppe and savannah, the Black-winged Kite, is to be found. In the *dehesas,* the cork oak country of the Portuguese *Alentejo* and the Spanish *Extremadura,* the harrier has found a perfect replica of an African savannah landscape. There are no owl species that especially inhabit the steppe, but the two all-rounders, the Little Owl and the Eagle Owl, are both to be found here. They nest in rocky crevices whenever possible but anything will do if these are not available; the great horned owl will even nest on the ground and the Little Owl often 'squats' the underground abodes of rodents.

Bird of the East European steppe: the Red-footed Falcon. This photo depicts a young bird.

A true element of African fauna in Europe: the Black-winged Kite. In the cork oak landscape of Spain and Portugal (the dehesas*) it has found the European equivalent of the African savannah.*

The breeding season

The life of birds of prey and owls is treated in two parts. In this chapter the breeding season is dealt with. It is a special period in the annual cycle of birds, which puts a heavy strain on them. This phase is not only about surviving, offspring have to be reared too. The season begins with pairing and marking out the territory. This is followed by building a nest, laying eggs and looking after the nestlings. The season ends with the chicks becoming independent. What happens after that is discussed in the following chapter, which deals with migration and wintering.

Buzzard's nest with little fluffy chicks.

Timing

The course of the breeding season is the same for all species of bird, but the timing and the duration of the process varies from one species to another. The differences are mainly determined by the food for the chicks: birds time their breeding season so that their young grow up in the period during which they can obtain the most food. Goshawks rear their young when the young starlings and young jays successively leave the nest. The chicks of mouse-eaters, like the buzzard and kestrel, grow up a little later, in the early summer when mice are at their most

Below: Montagu's Harriers make spectacular courtship flights, during which the male sometimes transfers the prey to the female. Even when the female starts to brood, she leaves the nest now and again to take, in full flight, prey which the male brings her.

Sometimes the partner and nesting place have to be defended against invaders. A male kestrel defends his nesting box and his partner against an invader, while the female recoils.

numerous and active. The chicks of species which eat a lot of insects, such as the hobby and Honey Buzzard, leave the nest in mid-summer. The Eleonora's Falcon rears its young in the autumn, when the migration of songbirds to Africa is at its height. These differences in species are genetically determined. Individuals which begin their breeding at exactly the right moment, produce more offspring than birds which are early or late; natural selection ensures that birds with good timing get the upper hand.

Within this average picture, there are variations in every species, per year, per area and per individual. In good years, when there is plenty of food, birds begin to breed earlier than in lean years; in good areas they begin earlier than in bad areas.

The condition of the female determines when she begins to lay eggs. This condition depends on the amount of food she had at the beginning of the breeding season. In years or in areas where there is a lack of food some pairs do not breed at all.

Pairing and marking out the territory

The breeding season begins with looking for a partner and marking out a territory. For the resident birds (in Western and Central Europe, for example the buzzard, goshawk and Tawny Owl) most of the pairs and territories are already decided in the early spring. The older birds usually breed in the same area every year and with the same partner. Empty places (through deaths) and new territories (of young birds) are partly already decided in the autumn and winter. In these species the activities directed towards procreation already begin in the course of the winter. In January and February the buzzard and goshawk pairs can be distinctly heard and seen, and Tawny Owls call continuously on bright, moonlit nights.

During an 'aerial battle' kestrels tumble over each other.

A female Montagu's Harrier with a twig for the nest.
The female usually builds the nest on her own.

The males of migratory birds usually return first; immediately after arrival they begin to mark out their territory and display courtship behaviour. Birds of prey show their presence by hovering over their territory and some patrol the borders regularly. Invaders are kept at a distance with threatening behaviour and, if necessary, driven away with physical violence. Owls mainly use vocal means. Male owls have a call which can be described as song. Although the sound is much simpler than that of songbirds, the function is exactly the same. The call of the Tawny Owl, well known from horror films, is an example of the owl's song. Through marking out the territory, the birds are equally distributed over an area, so that every breeding pair gets enough of the food supply.

Birds of prey and owls look for their food in a larger area outside the territory though, particularly when they have young. In this way they differ from songbirds, who have to rely on their own territory for food throughout the breeding season. This does not detract from the function of the territorial behaviour to prevent over-population.

In areas which are 'full' there are usually a number of individuals which do not occupy a territory and do not breed, although these birds are, in principle, capable of this. They are often immature birds. They form a reserve; as soon as a territory occupier drops out, the empty place is filled up by one of these birds. In growing populations, proportionately many young birds are excluded. The breeding success of younger birds is usually less than that of adults; they raise fewer young.

An even density is vital for species for which the sources of food are scattered. This applies to all owls and the majority of birds of prey, but there are a few exceptions among the birds of prey.

The nest of a Long-eared Owl. The Long-eared Owl does not build the nest itself, but uses old nests of other birds, usually crows.

The nest of a Montagu's Harrier on the ground in a wheat field.

Vultures, which live exclusively on carrion, breed in colonies. That is understandable, since one cadaver can supply a whole group of vultures and this group has the advantage that the birds can indicate the food sources to each other.

Also birds which are essentially insect-eaters, such as the Red-footed Falcon and the Lesser Kestrel, breed in colonies.

The courtship displays

The courtship displays of most birds of prey are usually accompanied by impressive demonstrations of flight: series of diving and soaring flights, looping the loop and somersaulting. Falcons engage in wild pursuits.

Harrier males make spectacular dives, during which they let themselves fall while turning around their own axis and appear to be going to crash, until, just above the ground, they flap their wings and rise again while calling loudly at the same time. Most spectacular are the colle-c-tive manoeuvres of the male and female, climaxing in the partners meeting each other in a mutual display, in which the male dives with lowered feet at the female, who turns over and raises her claws to him.

A female Marsh Harrier on the nest in reeds.

A Sparrow Hawk female on her nest in a forked branch of a birch. Sparrow Hawks do not usually brood high. They build their nests themselves, in fairly young trees, sometimes based on an old Sparrow Hawk nest or that of a Wood Pigeon.

Sometimes the male then gives a prey to the female. The ceremonial handing over of food by the male to the female (usually with less spectacle) is part of the courtship behaviour of many birds of prey and owls and has a clear function: later, when the female is sitting on the nest, the male has to provide her with food. Owls which live in open terrain during the day, such as the Snowy Owl and the Short-eared Owl, also have conspicuous courtship flights. For the nocturnal species, song plays a major part, in addition to other sounds such as special answering calls from the female and (in the case of the Long-eared Owl for example) clapping the wings and rattling the beak.

Nesting

When the territory is marked out and the pairs have been formed, nest building can begin. For some species 'nest' is an exaggeration: owls and falcons do not build a nest themselves. Many owls brood in caves and holes.

These can be natural cavities or woodpecker's holes in trees (Tawny Owl) or crevices in rocks (Eagle Owl) or openings in buildings (Barn Owl).

Various species, including the Tawny Owl and the Barn Owl, like special nesting boxes. Others, for ex-ample the Long-eared Owl, use the old nests of other birds, particularly those of crows. Some owl species, such as the Short-eared Owl, lay their eggs on the ground in a simple hollow with a few straws at the very most. Many falcons

Nest with young kestrels in a barn.

also brood in old crows' nests or the nests of other species. Some nest in and on buildings (the kestrel sometimes, the Lesser Kestrel mostly), in rock crev-ices or on ledges of rock (Peregrine). Kestrels also appreciate nesting boxes.

All other birds of prey build a nest themselves, sometimes with an existing nest from another bird as a basis.

Harriers brood on the ground, in fairly modest nests of stalks and other parts of plants. Large constructions would be too noticeable on the ground. Other birds of prey build nests of twigs

Brooding goshawk. The nest is 'decorated' with green twigs.

Sparrow Hawk's clutch of six eggs, more than average but not an unusual number. The eggs vary greatly in speckle pattern. They are hatched in about 40 days.

Following pages: The Eagle Owl often broods in rocky caverns.

in trees or on ledges of rock. These vary greatly in size, but are usually large in proportion to the size of the bird itself. Moreover, generally spe-aking, the bigger the bird of prey, the bigger (also in proportion!) its nest.

That principle culminates in the giant structure built by some large eagles, which a double bed would easily fit into.

The nests of birds of prey are often used more than once. Sometimes more nests can be found in one territory, from which one is selected. This can be the same nest as the year before, or an-other one.

The nest in use is decorated with green twigs. This makes it easy to determine whether a nest is occupied.

The male and female generally both take part in building the nest, but the female usually does most of the work. The female harrier does it alone; the goshawk males appear to do the lion's share. The time it takes to build a nest varies from less than a week (for harriers) to a few months.

Brooding

The number of eggs in a clutch varies greatly with birds of prey. The large vultures limit themselves to a single egg; harriers generally lay four to six eggs, but sometimes even ten. Broadly speaking, the rule is: the larger the bird, the fewer eggs, but this rule is not without exceptions. The Honey Buzzard, for example, lays fewer eggs (two) than another type of buzzard of the same size, while the hobby lays fewer (two or three) than the roughly equally-sized kestrel (generally four to six); harriers lay many eggs in

Left: a young buzzard exercises his wings.

Below: Barn Owls (as their name suggests) often brood in barns.

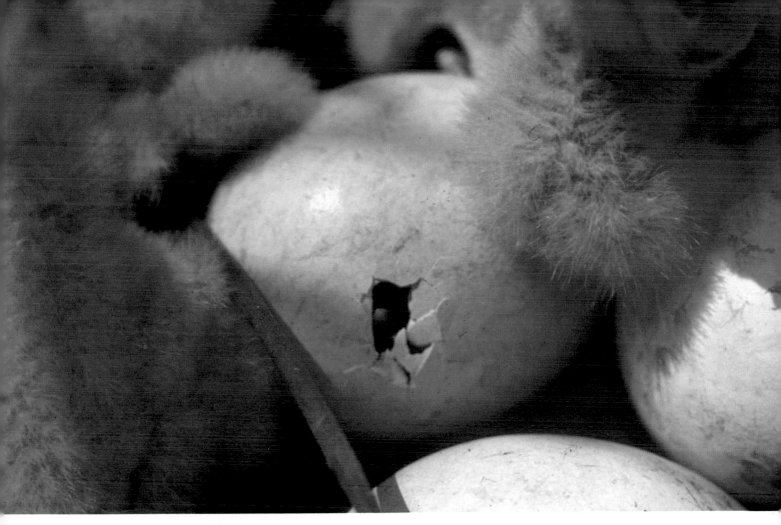

A young Marsh Harrier is busily breaking open its egg. The egg tooth can be clearly seen.

relation to their size. Owls generally lay fairly large clutches – larger than birds of prey of a similar size to themselves. The size of the clutch is roughly inversely proportional to the survival: the smaller the chance of survival for the adult birds, the more eggs are laid to compensate for this. The African migrants Honey Buzzard and hobby appear to have a greater chance of survival than the buzzard and kestrel who stay in Europe. Typical rodent-eaters such as the kestrel, the Rough-legged Buzzard and many owls vary the number of eggs they lay, from year to year. In years when there are plenty of mice they lay more eggs than in years with few mice.

The eggs of birds of prey differ in colour and speckle pattern; owls' eggs are white. This is usual in cave breeders; camouflage colours are not important to them, and white eggs show up better in the dark. But owls which brood in tree nests also lay white eggs, possibly because the camouflage of the bird sitting on the eggs is sufficient.

Most birds of prey and owls have a strict division of tasks: the female broods, the male takes care of the food. Kestrel males and the males of one or two other species, occasionally sit on the eggs, and the Honey Buzzard, as an exception to the rule, shares the tasks equally. For birds of prey and owls the incubation period is fairly long.

Fluffy young Montagu's Harrier.

The larger the species, the longer the incubation period. The tiny Scops Owl is the fastest with about 25 days. Most species take four to five weeks for the eggs to hatch, the large eagles take six weeks and vultures need even longer than seven weeks.

The young

Most birds do not begin to brood until the clutch is complete. Conversely, with most birds of prey the female begins to brood immediately after she has laid her first egg. The result of this is that the chicks differ in age and therefore have unequal chances of survival. The older and larger chicks beg more vigorously and get most of the food. The smaller ones do not get anything to eat until the bigger ones are satisfied and only survive if there is enough food. This is cruel in our eyes, but it is an effective way of ensuring the survival of the fittest.

With many birds of prey this principle goes so far that the stragglers only survive in very exceptional cases. In fact they constitute a reserve for times of plenty.

In some species, first-hatched chicks actively participate in the demise of the laggards by pecking them until they bleed and then working them to the edge of the nest or beyond. This is known as sibling killing.

A nest of young Hen Harriers, which differ considerably in size. It is usual in birds of prey that one or more young are stunted in growth. They usually do not survive the nest phase.

Birds of prey defend their broods fiercely against intruders. Here a researcher is attacked by a male Hen Harrier.

Left and below: the young Montagu's Harriers are looked after by both parents.

Distraction behaviour: a Short-eared Owl tries to entice the photographer away from the nest with young by simulating that his wings are damaged.

Below: young Short-eared Owls in the nest.

Right: a young Short-eared Owl with a fly.

The small, downy chicks cannot keep themselves warm in the beginning and have to be warmed regularly by the female. If this does not happen, they die. The male is now busier than ever with catching and bringing prey, which he gives to the female.

The female processes the bounty into tiny pieces, which she feeds to the young. This is a task exclusive to the females; in many species the males are even incapable of doing this. Cases have been known where the female died and the young starved to death, while the prey brought in by the male lay piled up in the nest, untouched.

After some time, when the chicks no longer need constant attention, the female goes out hunting again. The exact moment for this varies per species and per individual.

The most important cause of death among the nestlings is scarcity of food and bad weather (cold and rain).

Predation by other animals plays a subordinate part, but does occur. In such a case the culprit is often a fellow bird of prey or an owl. Birds of prey and owls defend their young fiercely against invaders.

Some do not shrink from attacking humans and this is not done gently!

Right: young Long-eared Owls: they have left the nest but are still looked after by their parents for a while. From dusk onward their plaintive, whistling begging call can be heard constantly.

Below: these young buzzards have grown a lot, here and there a tuft of down can be seen. Both fledglings have been ringed.

The claws of birds of prey, which strike with full power, can cause nasty injuries, as many a researcher and photographer have experienced. Such attacks are not limited to the larger species; the Tawny Owl is notorious in this respect. A bird photographer once lost an eye through a strike by a Tawny Owl! The Snowy Owl and the Short-eared Owl, species which brood on the ground in open terrain, do not resort to aggression but instead use distracting behaviour. They put on an act which is also seen among wading birds. They act as if they are wounded or cannot fly, in the hope of attracting attention to themselves and thus distract attention from the young. Quasi-helpless and with drooping wings, it limps ahead of the enemy and when it has coaxed him far enough away, the owl flies back and leaves the intruder behind, hoodwinked.

The young buzzard, a fledgling which has just left the nest, looks a bit absurd with the stray tufts of down.

Below: a young Long-eared Owl in threatening pose.

Young owls regularly leave the nest long before they can fly, and grub about in the direct vicinity. The young of birds of prey do this in the last few days before leaving the nest. The nesting period of the chicks is linked, just as the size of the clutch and the incubation period, to the size of the birds: the larger the species, the longer the fledglings remain in the nest. The Scops Owl takes three to four weeks to leave the nest, many birds of prey and owls take four to six weeks, the Golden Eagle ten weeks, and the large vultures nearly four months! After leaving the nest, the fledglings stay near their parents for some time and are fed by them – this period varies from three weeks for small species, to several months for large ones. They gradually learn to catch prey for themselves. Eventually the day comes when they can go their own way, independent of their parents.

The young Montagu's Harriers wait for food.

Below: the Montagu's Harriers have left the nest.

CHAPTER 7

Migration and wintering

After the breeding season has been concluded and the young birds have become independent, a relatively quiet period follows in the lives of birds of prey and owls. The important thing now is to survive and start the following spring in good condition. That would seem to be a considerably less demanding job than the rearing of offspring. But for birds of prey and owls, life is not as easy in the winter. Birds which spend the winter in northern regions, are confronted with smaller food stocks which get even smaller as the winter progresses. The conditions for hunting are less favourable, it takes a lot of effort to catch sufficient prey and in the winter especially energy is at a premium.

Three Griffon Vultures in their winter quarters in Africa, with a larger African relative, the Lappet-faced Vulture.

This period is the most difficult for first-year birds that do not yet have much experience. Those birds which choose to move to milder climes are confronted with the dangers of the journey.

The young birds are at a disadvantage here too: they arrive in unknown areas, in circumstances with which they are not familiar and partly with prey they do not yet know. Small wonder that the winter takes its toll of many first-year birds. By far the highest mortality among birds of prey

The Little Owl is a resident just like many other species of owl.

Below: the Scops Owl is the only real migrant among the European owls. Surprising for a sub-tropical breeding bird, but understandable because he mainly eats large insects and lizards. He finds these in Africa in the winter.

migratory bird among the owls. In the far north the merlin is a migrant. The small birds (song-birds in particular) which he hunts, are almost all summer visitors. In winter there is little for him to eat in the tundra and taiga. The Gyr Falcon, on the other hand, can survive the winter here on a diet of ptarmigan and so is predominantly a resident.

The Rough-legged Buzzard is a North European summer bird which lives on lemmings, mice and other small rodents. These are an irregular source of food, as a result of which some years more Rough-legged Buzzards migrate south than in others.

Below: some owls breeding in the north and living mainly on mice, such as the Short-eared Owl, migrate further some winters, always on the look-out for areas where mice are plentiful. A plague of mice can cause an invasion of Short-eared Owls.

and owls occurs in the first winter. The birds that get through this, have a much greater chance of survival.

Stay or migrate

The choice between staying in the breeding area or migrating depends largely on the food available. Birds with specialist food tastes, such as the Honey Buzzard and the Snake Eagle are explicitly long-distance migrants, that winter in Africa. This is obvious because in winter there are neither wasps nor snakes to be found in Europe.

All species which are wholly or partly dependent on insects, such as the Montagu's Harrier, hobby, Red-footed Falcon and Lesser Kestrel, winter in Africa. It is no coincidence, in view of his staple diet of insects, that, apart from the Short-eared Owl, the Scops Owl is the only

The fact that the Snake Eagle and the wasp-eating Honey Buzzard, winter in Africa is not difficult to understand, in view of their food preferences.

The majority of Black Kites migrate to Africa.

Owls are considerably less inclined to migrate than birds of prey. As we have already stated, the Scops Owl and the Short-eared Owl are the only real migrants among the European owls. The Long-eared Owl is a partial migratory bird; only the northern populations leave. The remaining ten species are all, more or less definite residents. There is a noticeable difference in the

A young White-tailed Eagle. In many species the young birds migrate further than the adults. Adult White-tailed Eagles normally stay in their breeding area.

northern coniferous forests. The birds of prey breeding there (goshawk, Sparrow Hawk, buzzard) leave in the winter, while the owls (Hawk Owl, Pygmy Owl, Ural Owl, Great Grey Owl, and Tengmalm's Owl) all stay. The difference in migratory behaviour between owls and birds of prey is partly to do with differences in the composition of their food. Owls are less specialised and more flexible in their choice of food than many birds of prey. They are more easily able to switch to another source of food when their preferred food is scarce. For want of mice for example, they switch over to birds. That is, however, not the most important explanation. In the taiga, songbirds are just as scarce for owls in winter as for birds of prey. Furthermore, there are birds of prey whose choice of food is at least as varied as that of the owls and who still migrate (harriers, kites). More important than the difference in the sort of food are the differences in getting it, which are linked to the way of hunting. Owls have the advantage because they can hunt perfectly by hearing. In this way they manage to make better use of the meagre supply. In Northern Europe in the winter, lemmings and voles are practically inaccessible to Rough-legged Buzzards and common buzzards, but owls manage to find them even under a layer of snow.

Right: Honey Buzzards wouldn't be able to find food in Europe in the winter. They are undeniable long-distance migrants, wintering deep inside Africa.

Furthermore, owls have the advantage that they can hunt during the day as well as by night. Thus in the short days of the northern winter they have much more time at their disposal than birds of prey, who have to gather all their food in the scanty hours of daylight.

Left: the Long-legged Buzzard is one of the eastern birds of prey that migrate along the coasts of the Middle East to Africa.

Below: just like many other birds of prey, Honey Buzzards migrate overland in order to take advantage of the warm air (thermals). That's why large concentrations can be seen in places where the crossing is shortest (Gibraltar, Bosporus).

The northern owl species are not pure residents, by the way. During most winters they remain at or near the breeding locations, but once every few years the Snowy Owl, Hawk Owl, Pygmy Owl and the Tengmalm's Owl 'erupt', during which the birds migrate from the breeding area in massive numbers. Such migratory explosions are typical for vole-eaters. Viewed over a longer period they display a cyclic pattern that is clearly connected to the changes in the mouse population. In periods when there are plenty of voles, the owls lay a lot of eggs and rear many chicks. When the vole population collapses, there is no longer enough food for all the birds and they leave the breeding area, in search of places where there is more to eat. The Short-eared Owl and the Rough-legged Buzzard, who are regular migrants anyway, also display these influxes.

Differences in migrating behaviour

Among birds of prey we find all variations of migratory behaviour, from pure residents to long-distance migrants. With the exception of the Gyr Falcon, residents can be found in Southern Europe: Bearded Vulture, Monk Vulture, Black-winged Kite, Lanner Falcon. Some migrants to Africa have already been mentioned, but the Black Kite, Egyptian Vulture, Pallid Harrier, Levant Sparrow Hawk, Lesser spotted Eagle, and

Buzzards are partially migratory. Breeding birds from Scandinavia migrate to Western and Central Europe, where they reinforce the numbers of their fellow-species there, who remain in their breeding area during winter.

Right: young hobby. Hobbies winter in South Africa. Their migration is inconspicuous: they cross the Mediterranean without hesitation, so they are seldom seen at the usual crossing-places for birds of prey.

The Montagu's Harrier winters in Africa.

Booted Eagle also spend the winters in Africa. Eleonora's Falcons winter on the island of Madagascar.

The real long-distance records, however, do not lie with the birds of prey. The Steppe Buzzard, the eastern sub-species of the buzzard, travels furthest: from Siberia to South Africa. Many

The Hen Harrier mainly migrates within Europe, but some birds fly on to North Africa.

birds of prey species remain largely inside Europe. Most of those are partial migrants, i.e. some populations migrate while others do not. The tendency to migrate decreases from north to south. Of the goshawk and Sparrow Hawk, only the northern populations migrate, in the rest of Europe they are residents.

The Marsh Harrier and the kite are migratory in the greater part of Europe, but the populations in the Mediterranean area remain there in win-

ter. There is sometimes also a distinct shift in migratory behaviour from east to west. This is most marked in the case of the buzzard, where the difference goes hand in hand with a division into two sub-species.

The western 'nominal' sub-species (say, the common buzzard) is a resident in a large part of his breeding area. The eastern sub-species, the Steppe Buzzard, is totally migratory, the majority of these winter in Southern Africa. The migration of the Steppe Buzzard probably has something to do with rivalry from the Rough-legged Buzzard, who winters in the breeding area of the Steppe Buzzard and has practically identical eating habits. Migrating to the west is not an option, because it is already full there with common buzzards, so he has little choice other than to divert to Africa. The differences between the two sub-species are adaptations to the difference in migratory behaviour: the western buzzard is heavier and lighter-coloured; the Steppe Buzzard is smaller and weighs less, and as a result, is a better long-distance flier.

In general, young birds travel farther than adults. For some partial migrants this amounts to the adult birds remaining in their breeding area and only the adolescent birds migrating. That applies, for example, to the North European White-tailed Eagle; which is why we nearly always see adolescent specimens here and rarely an adult bird (recognisable by the white tail). Such differences between young and old, often usual in many species, lead to the adult birds occupying the best spots and having the most chances for successful procreation.

Birds of prey migration

If you want to see something of the migration of birds of prey somewhere in inland Europe, you will need a lot of patience. In a few places, however, things are different: in Falsterbo, the southernmost point of Sweden, in Gibraltar and near Istanbul, every autumn bird-lovers from all

The migration of the Marsh Harrier takes place within Europe, but some specimens fly on to North Africa.

corners of the world throng to admire the stream of passing birds of prey. On a good day, without any trouble, you can see the passage of hundreds or even thousands of birds of prey. What these places have in common is that they form the point of access to the shortest possible ocean crossings. The birds cannot avoid these completely, although that is what the species who pass here in their thousands would prefer to do. They fly overland as much as possible, because they can then profit from the rising warm air. In columns of rising currents of warm air, they allow themselves to be carried, circling without wing-flapping, soaring up into the air and then again without flapping, making a descent over many kilometres until they find the next place where there are thermals. In this way they can travel great distances efficiently and without much loss of energy. Above the sea there are no thermals, so this strategy doesn't work there. The method is mostly used by typical 'gliding fliers', species with large, broad wings, such as buzzards and eagles. They are not built to travel long distances in normal flight. Species which are able to do that well, such as falcons and harriers, make little use of thermals. They just fly straight on to their destination, crossing the Mediterranean without hesitation. They are rarely seen at the previously-mentioned migration observation points.

The Honey Buzzard is somewhere in between these two groups; his build makes him suitable for both gliding and flapping flight. He opts for gliding where possible, and for normal flight where this is necessary (for example, during bad weather, without thermals).

Two other well-known concentration points of birds of prey migration lie outside Europe, but the birds largely come from there, just as the bird-watchers who come t• see and count the birds. One spot is the extreme northeast of Turkey, where birds of prey from the immense Russian hinterland pass in a narrow corridor between the Black Sea and the high mountains

The kestrel, a migratory bird within Europe. In severe winters which penetrate into the South European wintering areas, many kestrels die.

of the Caucasus. All these birds plus the migrants to Africa, having crossed the Bosporus at Istanbul, travel via a narrow corridor along the east coast of the Mediterranean over Lebanon and Israel in the direction of Africa. They arrive there at the ultimate 'hot spot': Eilat, the southernmost point of Israel.

In Africa

The birds of prey migrating to Africa, generally winter in the savannah to the north of the jungle belt (the Sahel; harriers, for example) or to the south of this (for example, the hobby and the Red-footed Falcon). Food is not plentiful there. Many birds of prey, therefore, have no fixed winter residence, but lead a roving existence. They search out the spots with temporary concentrations of food, where they hunt in groups, often with several species together. Places like these are, for instance, the edges of fires, where all kinds of animals (insects, mammals, birds) are disturbed by the fire, and places where it has rained. Hobbies follow the rain fronts where the termites swarm out in masses.

The trouble which birds of prey have to go to, in order to find food and the distances they have to travel for this, explains why they don't stay in Africa the whole year, but in the spring start the return journey to the north, to the temporary summer abundance there.

The winter in Europe

The birds of prey and owls that stay in Europe during the winter, do not have an easy time either. The supply of food dwindles, the prey creep away and are inaccessible, or more difficult to catch because they live in groups. Hunting takes more energy because weather conditions are often unfavourable, and in the winter it is best to expend as little energy as possible. The birds react to this by enlarging their action radius. In contrast to their relatives in Africa, they usually maintain a fixed hunting territory. Residents often remain in their own breeding area, but hunt in a

Many birds of prey and owls lead a fairly solitary life in general, but outside the breeding season they are sometimes a bit more social. Long-eared Owls spend the day at collective sleeping places, often well-hidden in evergreen trees and bushes, like this holly.

larger area around it. They adjust their choice of terrain too. Buzzards and goshawks, who breed in forests, hunt more in open terrain where there is more to catch in the winter. In periods of frost, Sparrow Hawks travel along with their prospective prey – small songbirds – to towns and villages. Just as in Africa, birds of prey and owls can also be found here in groups; although this doesn't mean very much. It usually concerns opportune connections in places where there is a lot of food. These connections break up again just as easily. More permanent group connections are the communal sleeping places which the Hen Harrier and the Long-eared Owl frequent. Long-eared Owls sleep during the day close together in groups, ranging from a few to dozens of birds, in one tree or a few trees, often a conifer or some other evergreen species. Such 'roosting places' are sometimes used for years on end. The most important function of communal sleeping places is probably safety. Whether or not they are important for the transfer of information about food is doubtful, because most birds hunt individually and drive others away from their hunting area.

CHAPTER 8

Birds of prey and man

Birds of prey have very few natural enemies. There is only one species of animal which they really fear: man. From time immemorial people have really had it in for birds of prey. For centuries they have been portrayed as 'vermin' and persecuted with every means possible. As a result of this, many birds of prey have become rare and have disappeared from large areas of Europe. The cutting down of forests and reclamation of swamps, fens and steppes have not done most of the birds of prey and owls any good either. Nowadays, birds of prey are protected by law almost everywhere, but the persecution continues illegally. Add to that shooting birds of prey for fun, trapping them for falconry, the loss of sources of food and breeding biotope, particularly in Southern Europe and Eastern Europe, and the indirect poisoning through pesticides used in agriculture, and it will become clear that things don't look rosy for birds of prey. Fortunately, there are also positive developments. A number of species are on the increase in some areas and campaigns are being organised to protect birds of prey and re-introduce them in areas from where they had disappeared.

Research is necessary to be able to protect birds of prey effectively.

Persecution

The persecution of birds of prey reached a doubtful high spot in the nineteenth century and the beginning of the twentieth century. During this period, interest in shooting increased and people began to breed and set out pheasants. Birds of prey took advantage of this new source of food and that was their downfall. The human hunter does not tolerate competitors. Birds of prey were vermin and had to be exterminated. The persecution was encouraged by the authorities and took on inconceivable proportions. Many birds of prey were killed in order to collect premiums.

No distinction was made between species and birds of prey were blamed for all kinds of things by people who had little or no knowledge of the facts.

The witch-hunt against these birds not only came from the hunters, but also from conservationists. They saw birds of prey as a threat to the animals they wanted to protect.

In the course of the twentieth century people began to realise that birds of prey do not endanger the population of their quarry and that their alleged status as vermin was not supported

Birds of prey and owls (in the photo a Long-eared Owl) are often traffic victims.

by facts (see chapter 4). This insight gradually won ground with the authorities and laws were passed protecting birds of prey. Nowadays, birds of prey are formally protected nearly everywhere in Europe, but in spite of this, (illegal) persecution still continues in many places. For this no holds are barred. Birds of prey are shot, killed with poisoned bait, caught in traps and kept in cages. Nests are riddled with shot, removed and destroyed and sometimes whole nesting trees are sawn or chopped down.

In Southern and Eastern Europe many people would rather see a dead bird of prey than a live one. But also in countries nearer home, the persecution of birds of prey is a widespread and again increasing phenomenon.

Shooting circles are mainly responsible for this, where birds of prey are still seen as competitors

A falconer on an airfield with a peregrine on his hand. This is evidence that a trained bird of prey does good work in frightening and driving away other birds, so that collisions with aircraft can be avoided..

In the bazaars in Istanbul Sparrow Hawks are offered for sale as pets.

Thanks to their 'human' features owls have always had a better image than birds of prey. Many farmers welcome Barn Owls; they are regarded as being 'useful' because they eat mice.

and persistent prejudices triumph over knowledge.

Owls have had less trouble from systematic persecution. They have never been stamped as 'wicked villains'. Perhaps their nocturnal way of life has been to their advantage, and made extermination more difficult. In any case, the fact that they kill mice may have something to do with it.

And yet, owls have not entirely escaped persecution and, intentionally or unintentionally, may have become a victim of the human urge to destroy. The witch-hunt that took place all over Europe did not miss its goal. Large species, in particular, were the victims. They are an easy

Young goshawks. Few birds of prey have suffered so much at the hands of man as the goshawk, described as 'dangerous vermin' and seen by the hunter as a rival.

target and because they are scattered and occur in small numbers, the effect on the size of their population is, in proportion, great.

The current scattered distribution pattern of the White-tailed Eagle and the osprey are the result of human intervention. In the course of the nineteenth and the twentieth centuries they have been exterminated in Western Europe: Great Britain, the Netherlands and Denmark. Vultures can now practically only be found in Southern Europe, but once the Bearded Vulture, the Monk Vulture and the Griffon Vulture also occurred in large parts of central Europe, and in France, Germany, Switzerland, Austria and the Czech Republic.

Although vultures rarely or never attack living animals, they were lumped together with other birds of prey. In addition, they were victims of the laying of poisoned bait, intended for other birds and for foxes and wolves. In the Balkans, which used to be a paradise for birds of prey, the numbers of eagles and vultures have been decimated.

The effect of persecution on smaller, more numerous species is difficult to prove, because we don't know how large the numbers were in the past. That they have decreased through persecution is highly likely, if only through the numbers of dead birds of prey which were handed in during that time, and which cannot be visualised in the current population. One indication is also the increase in birds of prey during the two world wars, which has been mentioned in various sources.

Left: young Imperial Eagles exercise their wings. Large birds of prey like the Imperial Eagle have become rare and timid through centuries of intensive persecution.

The persecution ceased temporarily then, because people had other things on their minds and weapons were being used for other purposes.

Loss of habitat

Persecution is not the only cause of the decline in birds of prey – possibly not even the most important. Loss of habitat has also played a large part. Cutting down the original forests and the reclamation of peat moors and swamp areas has caused species such as the White-tailed Eagle, the Lesser spotted Eagle and the Spotted Eagle to disappear. Their decline started centuries ago. Such large birds of prey are sensitive to the frag-

There is no end to the lengths some people will go to exterminate birds of prey. If they do not succeed in killing the birds or getting to the nest to take the eggs, they can saw down the tree, nest and all!

A few centuries ago the White-tailed Eagle occurred in large parts of Europe, but by merciless persecution there are now only a few left in remote areas. Now conservationists are trying to get the White-tailed Eagle back again by releasing birds imported from Norway.

mentation of the landscape. They need large, connected, unspoilt nature reserves, in which various landscapes (wood, water and swamp) are all present. In today's landscape, with its scattered remnants of nature, there is no place for them. The harrier and the Short-eared Owl, who do not need such large hunting areas, were able to support themselves for a long time in the scattered, smaller swamps and moors that remain. But for them also, the point of no return has now been reached and their numbers are declining fast. Due to the large-scale recla-mation of the steppes in Eastern Europe, birds of prey such as the Long-legged Buzzard, the Pallid Harrier, the Tawny Eagle and the Saker Falcon, have lost much ground. The process continues to this day.

Sparrow Hawk with young. Around 1970 the Sparrow Hawk nearly became extinct due to the use of virtually non-biode-gradable pesticides. After the most damaging ones had been forbidden, the numbers recovered.

Pesticides

In addition to the insidious decline through per-secution and loss of habitat, a new acute threat appeared in the 1960's. In various countries in Western Europe, in the years between 1950 and 1970, many birds of prey were suddenly found dead. The suspicion that poisoning could be the cause of death, was soon confirmed by tests. The birds' corpses proved to contain fatal doses of substances which were used in agriculture as pesticides.

Through the disappearance of natural forests and the reclamation of swamps, the Spotted Eagle has lost much of its habitat.

The greatest culprits were insecticides and fungicides mainly used to disinfect seed for sowing. Birds of prey were absorbing these substances via their prey, which in turn had taken them in via their food.

With each step in the food chain, the concentration of poison increases because the toxins are not broken down in the body. Since birds of prey are the last link in the food chain, they were the victims. The poison collected in the fatty tissue and death followed, particularly in the winter when the birds started to use their fat reserves.

Direct mortality was not the only effect of the pesticides on birds of prey. In the same period it was established more frequently that the eggs produced by birds of prey more often had thin shells, as a result of which the eggs broke. DDT proved to be mainly responsible for this. Birds also sometimes sat on eggs which did not hatch because the embryos were dead, and chicks died from poisoning.

The consequences soon became apparent. In Great Britain the numbers of Sparrow Hawks, merlins and peregrines fell to an unprecedented low level.

In North America and other European countries a decline in various species of birds of prey was also ascertained. When it became apparent that a disaster was in progress, most applications of the substances in question were prohibited. In Western Europe the populations of buzzard, goshawk, Sparrow Hawk and peregrine quickly recovered.

This does not mean that the problems with poisons used in agriculture are completely over.

Below: some owls brood in nesting-boxes. The mirror enables us to see who the occupier is (Ural Owl) and what is happening in the nesting-box.

The current insecticides in use have no apparent consequences, but there are indications that with certain species more insidious processes are involved.

Furthermore, the substances which are prohibited in the western world are being freely used in other parts of the world and in Africa in particular.

The consequences for birds of prey wintering in Africa are as yet unknown, but it is likely that there will be effects. Ultimately, the use of pesticides means a decline in food supplies, for insect-eaters in particular.

Current threats

Now that they have come through the crisis of the pesticide attack, the buzzard, the Sparrow Hawk and the goshawk seem to be holding their own well in cultivated landscapes with scattered woods. That also applies to species such as the Honey Buzzard and the Long-eared Owl, which have continued to be unaffected by all malaise. With other species, however, which

breed or look for food in cultivated landscape areas, things are not going so well.

In Eastern and Southern Europe, in particular, some species are in trouble because the traditional varied cultivated landscape is being replaced by large-scale intensive farming. The most poignant example is the Lesser Kestrel. Thirty years ago this species was numerous and it is now threatened with extinction. It has already disappeared from Poland, the Czech Republic, Slovakia and Hungary, where until quite recently it was a perfectly common bird. In Southern Europe the same thing happened: in Spain in 1990 there was at the most only one fifth, possibly even only one tenth of the number

Below: a young Sparrow Hawk. Fortunately, things are going a little better for this species of bird of prey.

Following pages: a brooding goshawk female. The teardrop-shaped markings on the breast show that it is a young bird. Young birds breeding is an indication of disturbed population composition – the result of persecution by humans. In stable populations breeding occurs almost exclusively by adult birds.

occurring in 1980. The problem for the Lesser Kestrel lies in the loss of extensive meadowlands, where he finds his food, which consists of large insects such as grasshoppers. These traditional grasslands are making way for large-scale arable farming and afforestation. This also has harmful consequences for the Snake Eagle and the Bonelli's Eagle.

Even familiar sights in the cultivated landscape in practically the whole of Europe, like the kestrel, the Barn Owl and the Little Owl, are threatened as a result of the advancing modernisation and economies of scale in agriculture. As a result of hedges, wooded banks and old-fashioned orchards being cleared away, their breeding places are being lost, and they can find less and less food on the intensively-farmed agricultural land. In large areas of Europe their numbers are declining. In addition, birds of prey are being confronted with a series of other threats. In a number of southern countries, large numbers of birds are being shot for fun. It's true that this is illegal in most cases, but traditions die hard in these countries and there is little control. Southern France, Malta, Italy, Greece, Cyprus and Turkey are notorious. In Italy the hunt for Honey Buzzards is a national sport. The rich Arabs' love of falconry forms a threat to the Lanner Falcon, Saker Falcon, Peregrine Falcon and Gyr Falcon. Young birds are stolen from the nests to provide falcons for enthusiasts of this popular sport in the Middle East. The oil sheikhs pay high prices for these desirable birds.

Barn Owls and Little Owls like to search for their food along road-sides, which often results in their falling victim to the traffic. In Eastern Europe many birds of prey die in collision with electricity cables and by electrocution on electricity pylons, which the birds like to use as a look-out post, particularly in open steppe country.

Saker Falcons are very popular in the Arab world for falconry. Enormous sums of money are paid for them, leading to thousands of Saker Falcons being caught each year as chicks or during migration.

The increase in more adventurous forms of recreation, such as walking in the mountains, is a problem for species such as the Spotted Eagle, the Imperial Eagle and the Eagle Owl, which are extremely sensitive to being disturbed and desert the nest if people come too close.

Protection

On balance, the European birds of prey are not really in a good way. The numbers of various species are but a fraction of what they were, some are on the verge of extinction. It is the same story for other species which, until recently, were numerous. Fortunately, there are some rays of hope. Threatened species, such as the White-tailed Eagle, the Bearded Vulture, the Monk Vulture, the Griffon Vulture, the osprey

The Lesser Kestrel is disappearing fast, along with the varied cultivated landscape in which he feels at home. The large-scale modern farming areas, which have replaced them, have nothing to offer him.

The Lanner Falcon has less than 250 pairs in the whole of Europe and is one of the most seriously threatened species of bird of prey.

and the peregrine, are again increasing in number; in a part of their breeding area in any case. That is largely due to special protective measures. In opposition to those who hate birds of prey there is a growing group of people who put their hearts and souls into improving the replaced their fate.

On the whole there is no lack of legal protection. Of course protection on paper is a minimum condition, but it is certainly not enough. We have seen that the illegal hunting down of birds of prey continues unabated. Everything depends on good maintenance and monitoring of the law, and a change in attitude. The latter requires good propaganda. Voluntary groups are active to this end. They work with gamekeepers and police to take stock of the persecution of birds of prey, bringing this to the attention of the public and improving the image of these birds. In other countries too, monitoring and information supply are important parts of the work of protection.

The kestrel is a very common sight nowadays. It is a bird of prey that seems to have adapted itself to humans. And yet, this bird is declining in many places due to the intensity and economies of scale in agriculture.

Below: the osprey has returned to Scotland, thanks to intensive protection, which included volunteers guarding the nests day and night. The nests have now become a tourist attraction.

In addition, nests are sometimes actually physically protected. Hundreds of volunteers are involved in guarding the nests, literally day and night. The successful come-back of the osprey in Scotland would not have been possible without permanently guarding the nests against vandals who tried their hardest to sabotage this success. It looks as though the tide has now turned, however, and the ospreys have become a tourist attraction. In Germany the nests of osprey and peregrine are guarded 24 hours a day and in Hungary they have successfully put a stop to the plundering of the nests of Saker Falcons.

Sometimes the birds are helped with artificial nesting-places. Nesting-boxes are eagerly used by kestrels and by some owls. For each species there are specific models.

In Holland the Barn Owl population, which was dangerously near the minimum, has been boosted by placing special nesting-boxes in farmer's barns. Success has been booked in locations in Germany, with artificial nesting platforms for ospreys on high-tension masts, and in Hungary this has been done for Saker Falcons. The Hungarians have, in addition, helped the Saker Falcons by releasing sousliks, their most important prey, in places where these had disappeared.

The most drastic form of protection is to release birds of prey again in areas where they have disappeared. A successful example of this is the re-introduction of the Griffon Vulture in the area of the *causses* in the Massif Central in France. In 1981, forty years after the species had become extinct, the first birds were set out. They came from bird sanctuaries, where they had recovered from poisoning or injury, and from zoos. Each year a few birds were released; others bred in large aviaries in the introduction area. Their offspring were also released in the area. The birds, living free, set up a colony and soon began to display their natural behaviour. After a few years they also began to breed in the wild and meanwhile the population is able to maintain itself.

The only help they still receive from humans is additional feeding. At fixed locations ('vulture restaurants') slaughterhouse waste is put down for them. This is necessary because what used to be their natural source of food has disappeared: roaming herds of cattle have be-come a rarity

In Oost-Groningen (the Netherlands) the nests of Montagu's Harriers are tracked down in fields so that the young birds can be saved during harvest.

Following pages: through hunting and poisoning the Egyptian Vulture is fast declining in number.

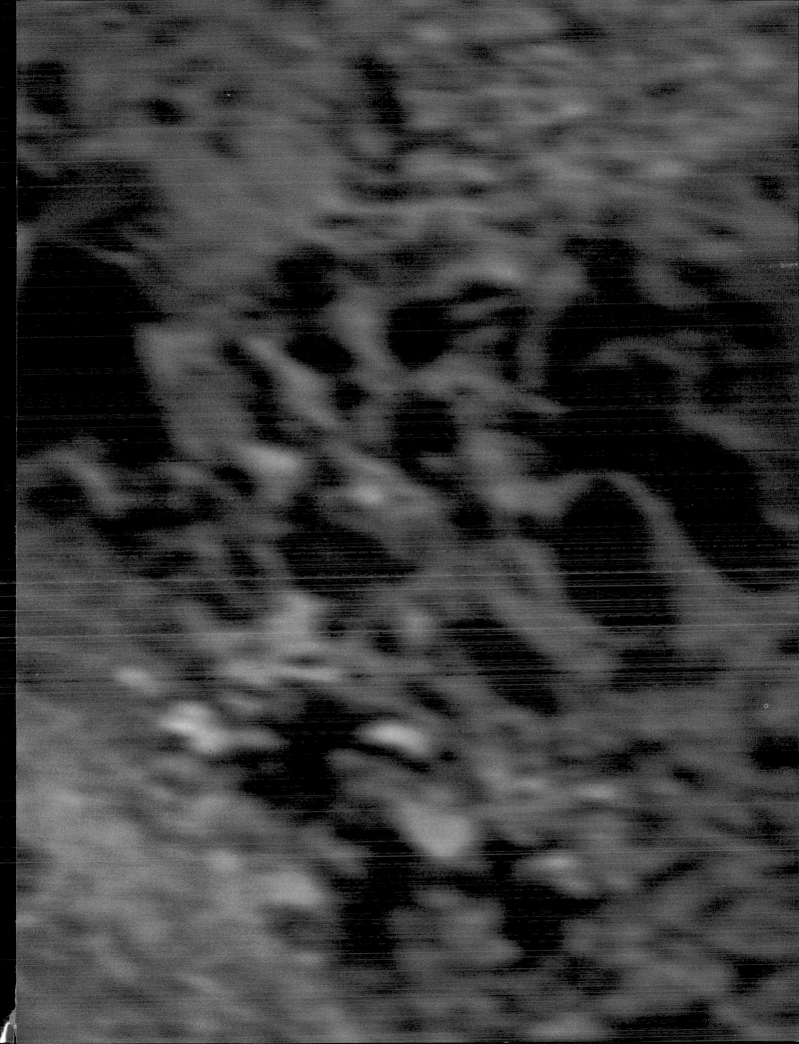

The Red Kite has been re-introduced into Wales, but he is not yet accepted by everyone. Some birds are still being shot and poisoned.

Sometimes birds of prey protection goes very far. Here, the nest of a Montagu's Harrier is protected from foxes by electrified wire. In a 'natural' situation this would be unnecessary, but when a species is teetering on the brink of extinction, cunning tricks are justified.

and cadavers have to be cleared away by law. The re-introduction was accompanied by an intensive propaganda campaign. In the past, vultures were shot and poisoned by the local people because of their alleged damage to livestock. People believed, for instance, that, the swooping vultures frightened the cattle, causing them to fall into a ravine. Now it is known that vultures do no harm, they have become very popular.

Stimulated by the success with the Griffon Vulture, the French bird protectors have begun a similar re-introduction of the Monk Vulture, experience of which has been gained in Majorca in the last few years. In the Alps, Bearded Vultures which grew up in captivity have been set out.

In Scotland a small population of White-tailed Eagles is breeding again, thanks to the re-introduction of birds from Norway. Red Kites have been brought into various locations in Britain and are now breeding successfully. In other

places too, there are projects or plans for the re-introduction of birds of prey.

All these actions are good and useful, but not enough. The most important condition for the continuing existence of birds of prey and owls is that their habitat is maintained. Protected nature reserves are essential for this. Particularly in the eastern part of Europe, where large, relatively intact areas can be found that are threatened by advancing 'civilisation', the establishment of nature reserves can contribute a great deal. But nature reserves alone are not enough to save birds of prey and owls. Wise management is necessary for our whole environment, including the non-protected areas. Most urgent of all is to reflect on the way in which we treat our agrarian landscape.

Right: birds of prey which have been shot, wounded, or weakened are patched up by members of the bird protection society and then released.

Below: the young Lesser Spotted Eagle makes a fresh start.

Things will have to change pretty quickly, or we will soon lose the Lesser Kestrel and the same applies for his bigger brother.

INDEX

Left: the Griffon Vulture was completely exterminated in France, but in the Cévennes it has been successfully re-introduced.

Acknowledgements

Theo Bakker, Groningen, the Netherlands: pages 88 above right, 135 top

Leo Boon, Groningen, the Netherlands: pages 7, 8 top, 9, 10-11, 12, 14, 15, 18 top, 19 below, 22 below right, 23 right, 26-27, 34, 36 below, 39, 42, 43 left, 44, 46 left, 47 below, 51, 52 top, 54 left, 58 below, 59 top, 60 top, 76 top, 78, 79 left, 81, 82, 86 right, 88 below, 89, 90 above left, 91 below, 100-101, 110-111, 112, 114, 115 above right and left, 126, 130, 131, 134, 135 below, 136 below, 141, 142, 143 right and below

J. Boshuizen, Amsterdam, the Netherlands: pages 45 below, 53, 103 top, 125 top

Koen van Dijken, Groningen, the Netherlands: pages 43 right, 56-57, 115 below

Jan van Holten, Schiedam, the Netherlands: page 90 below left

Hans Hut, Ten Boer, the Netherlands: pages 4, 6, 8 below, 13, 16-17, 18 below, 19 top, 20-21, 22 left and above right, 23 left, 24, 25, 28, 29, 30, 31, 32-33, 35, 36 top, 37, 38, 40-41, 45 top, 46 right, 47 top, 48-49, 50, 52 below, 54 top and right, 55, 58 right, 59 below, 60 below, 61, 62, 63, 64-65, 66, 67, 68, 69, 70-71, 72, 73, 74, 75, 80 left, 83, 84-85, 86 left and below, 87, 88 above left, 90 below right, 91 top, 92-93, 94, 95, 96-97, 98, 99, 102, 103 below, 104, 105, 106, 107, 108, 109, 113 below, 116, 117, 118, 119, 120, 121, 122-123, 124, 125 below right and left, 127, 128, 129, 132-133, 136 top, 137, 138-139, 140, 143 left

Eric Koops, Groningen, the Netherlands: pages 76 below, 77, 79 right, 113 top

J. v.d. Leigraaf, Huissen, the Netherlands: page 58 left